BRINGING HISTORY TO LIFE

First-person Historical Presentations in Elementary and Middle School Classrooms

Ronald Vaughan Morris

ROWMAN & LITTLEFIELD EDUCATION
Lanham • New York • Toronto • Plymouth, UK

Published in the United States of America
by Rowman & Littlefield Education
A Division of Rowman & Littlefield Publishers, Inc.

A wholly owned subsidiary of The Rowman & Littlefield Publishing Group, Inc.
4501 Forbes Boulevard, Suite 200, Lanham, Maryland 20706
www.rowmaneducation.com

Estover Road
Plymouth PL6 7PY
United Kingdom

British Library Cataloguing in Publication Information Available

Library of Congress Cataloging-in-Publication Data
Morris, Ronald V.
  Bringing history to life : first-person historical presentations in elementary and
middle school classrooms / Ronald Vaughan Morris.
     p. cm.
  Includes index.
  ISBN 978-1-60709-223-0 (cloth : alk. paper)—ISBN 978-1-60709-224-7
(pbk. : alk. paper)—ISBN 978-1-60709-225-4 (electronic)
  1. History—Study and teaching (Elementary) 2. History—Study and teaching
(Middle school) 3. Social history—Study and teaching (Elementary) 4. Social
history—Study and teaching (Middle school) 5. Historical reenactments. 6.
One-person shows (Performing arts) I. Title.
  D16.25.M67 2009
  372.89—dc22
                                                                    2009001500

⊗ ™ The paper used in this publication meets the minimum requirements of
American National Standard for Information Sciences—Permanence of Paper
for Printed Library Materials, ANSI/NISO Z39.48-1992.
Manufactured in the United States of America.

Contents

List of Tables

Acknowledgments

MANY PEOPLE HAVE CONTRIBUTED TO the success of this book, and I am very pleased to be able to thank them. Martha Morris reviewed and critiqued multiple drafts of this manuscript; she is always conscientious and good-humored. As my mom and a college professor, she has performed this task for years, and I am extremely grateful. She reviewed the first thing I remember writing, which was a second-grade script for a play about Jamestown; she will always be my favorite editor. In retirement she still has a keen eye for areas in my writing that require clarification and redevelopment.

The last chapter I wrote is actually based on one of my longest educational associations. Glen Dillman and I met in 1975 in a history enrichment program. For many years he has provided a source of inspiration, investigation, and dedication to not only me, but to countless students who pass through his classes, his peers, and the members of his community. His ideas of artifacts, first-person presentation, and social studies enrichment informed my early teaching and mentored my development as an educator. He was named Daughters of the American Revolutions and Indiana's Teacher of the Year in 1984, served as a Master Teacher in Residence at Purdue University, and has received a Fulbright Scholarship to China and Indiana Council for the Social Studies Teacher of the Year in 2008.

I had the pleasure of meeting Barbara Johnson in the early 1980s. Her passion for state and local history led her to move and manage a schoolhouse; maintain, develop, and interpret a local history museum; and provide rich extracurricular social studies experiences for students. Barb graciously opened her classroom for some of my early social studies research projects. Her advice on interactive social studies experiences for middle-grade elementary students really helped to shape my ideas about best teaching practices.

Jean McNeely, a National Council for the Social Studies Outstanding Elementary Teacher, graciously opened her classroom to me on several research projects while I was in Texas. She introduced me to the local history of the area, and she helped to interest so many of her students in the history of their state through study travel and creative drama experiences. She absolutely loved to help her students see the obvious connections to national events, and she enjoyed connecting them to the land and culture of their home.

Many other elementary social studies teachers provided interviews and advice that shaped this work, but space does not allow me to include them all. Nadine Roush, whom I had the pleasure of meeting while at Purdue University, graciously opened her classroom to me for several research projects. Brian Fouts helped me to find out more about a young teacher who was experimenting with elementary social studies education and first-person presentation.

Thanks to Wendy for organizing the photo shoot and thanks to Brenda Havens of Digital Runes for the cover art. Thanks to Carla, Chase, Diamond, Elaine, Emily, Katherine, Krystal, Leah, Michael, Molly, Patricia, and Timothy for assisting with the cover art.

Thanks go to Diane, Shelley, and Marsha at Ball State University's Department of History for their support and good humor. Thanks are given to the editors of *Gifted Child Today* and *Social Studies and the Young Learner* who extended permission to use articles previously printed in their journals. Thanks also go to the blind reviewers of this manuscript. Finally, my thanks go to Patti Belcher, my gracious editor at Rowman Education; she always had good ideas.

Introduction

READERS OF THIS BOOK LEARN HOW teachers and students use first-person historical presentations in the elementary and middle school social studies classrooms. They learn how to create first-person presentations with their students by discovering many examples across the various grades. Real classroom teachers and students illustrate this book best when they use first-person presentations in their social studies classrooms from second to eighth grade. The topic of first-person presentations is of increasing importance due to the suppression of field trips to popular museums that interpret history by using this method. While different from a field trip, the first-person presentation allows people to interact with different characters from history and helps them consider differing perspectives.

In writing this book, I drew on my eight years of classroom experience as an elementary school teacher, twelve years of leading elementary-level enrichment experiences, and lifelong experiences of working with local historical societies. I also have fifteen years of teaching college students to help primarily elementary- and middle-school social studies classroom teachers work with students who are developing first-person presentations. Through in-service workshops or social studies methods classes, teachers create their own first-person presentations. Teachers move from their research and presentation to focus on student research, presentation, and application. Recipients of the Teaching American History Grant have sparked renewed interest in this method. Museum educators—those who work in cultural institutions, such as libraries, preservation societies, historical societies, and public interpretation—use this book to improve their first-person presentations with both students and visitors.

First-person presentations are good for students because they can help both teachers and students work with value-based social studies instruction. Students engage with historical empathy as they come to understand a character, the context of their time, and their peers. Students examine controversial issues as the content of their studies rather than just reciting a litany of facts. Students look at multiple points of view surrounding controversial issues, including both sides of the issue. Students work with alternative perspectives of the views and ideas represented by people who are often excluded from debates or narratives. Students examine the issues and render a moral judgment to determine if the results of the issue were good for individuals, good for groups, or good for society.

The scope of the book follows the growth of the students through the social studies curriculum; chapters two through eight correspond with the second through eighth grades. The first chapter includes an overview of the use of first-person presentation and points to many places where people have seen first-person presentations being used successfully. In this chapter I help the teachers set up their own first-person presentations and establish the context for the various case studies explored in the rest of the book. Second-grade students work with a holiday to learn about a president while connecting to their culture. Third-grade students learn about their community and social history when they spend a day in a one-room school. Fourth-grade students work with multiple perspectives and labor with their state studies curriculum to see how a first-person presentation connects to the rest of their curriculum. Fourth- and fifth-grade teachers work to direct attention, encourage involvement, give assessment, and establish context with the American Revolution. Sixth-grade students work with research, preparation, and connection with their community before engaging with younger students in the elementary school next door. Seventh-grade students work with multicultural content to present first-person presentations in groups to younger students who work with economics and geography. Eighth-grade students learn about American studies by working with a variety of characters and artifacts that provide retention, context, and a unique experience for the purpose of examining existential ideas. In the concluding chapter, I reflect upon the lessons learned from each of these case studies and explain how the implications for teachers and museum educators further illustrate the usefulness of this method. In-service teachers apply this type of teaching to their classrooms to cover standards and to provide enrichment. The experience of using this method improves teaching and learning in classrooms and tells how museums can apply these lessons to visitors. Finally, the implications for students doing their own first-person presentations show that social studies students do profit from using the method.

Chapter One

─────────○─────────

Introduction to First-person Presentation

A FIRST-PERSON HISTORICAL CHARACTER is defined as either an actual person like John Muir, a composite person who is drawn from several real sources such as a pioneer woman, or an inanimate object like the Statue of Liberty. The interpreter talks as if he or she is that person using I, my, mine, and me so that the audience believes that the person could really be the character they are portraying. Many times the interpreter wears period clothing and has props from the time in question. They may affect an accent from the time or location and use period words, slang, phrases, and idioms. They try to help the audience find out about a specific time, place, people, group, or idea.

You may have seen people using first-person historical presentations at various places quite successfully. The National Park Service introduced me to John Muir in a California campground during an evening program; the audience, which was completely mesmerized, asked questions until the original one-hour program stretched into nearly three hours. You may have seen a homily delivered in the first person with a shepherd describing the Christmas story. You may have traveled to living history museums such as Plymouth Plantation, a living history farm, or a historical site such as Conner Prairie to meet people who are interpreting the past. Your children's librarian may dress up like the Cat in the Hat;

actors often create one-man shows around Mark Twain or Harry Truman, and of course teachers often do this, too.

I wanted my students to experience social studies both in the classroom and in the world. I engaged a lot of guest speakers who could come into the school and tell the students about life in the past. This worked really well and helped the community feel that this was their school, but that is the topic for another book. Guest speakers could take us back to the beginnings of the twentieth century, but that was as far as they could go. When I could not get a person who could take my students into the nineteenth century, I needed another way for my students to experience the past.

As a young teacher I needed to incorporate social studies objectives that would help my students to both understand time and explain how people changed across time. Most of the first-person characters that I impersonated started with the objectives, research, and an outline of topics plus a prop to help my students realize that I had become someone else. Dr. Granny was a good example of this approach; the objective was to help students define what Granny cures were and to explain how people still occasionally use folk medicine rather than going to the doctor. My research included a list of ailments and folk cures; I used a slouch hat that held pieces of paper with many of the ailments printed on them. As the students selected an ailment from the hat, Dr. Granny then put the hat on his head and went around the room telling the students what they needed to do to be cured.

The Dr. Granny character never needed to be developed more than that. The War of 1812 freshwater sailor, however, wore a $1.25 sailor suit from a flea market and was a character that did grow over the years. It is permissible to start small and build the presentation, character, and content over time. Some of my characters, such as George Mason, became very complex with historic clothing, props, primary sources, and artifacts. In reality you do not need props, but you do need a good imagination. The props only help you trigger that imagination in both you and in your students.

Preparing to talk about my grandfather on the home front during World War II or my great grandfather during World War I required me to do some of the easiest research. It was just a matter of talking to them or to other relatives in order to get details that would personalize the story for the home front. My period clothes were readily available, as were all the photos, primary sources, and artifacts that I could carry. Family history also provided me with the story of Captain John Doyle, who marched with General George Rogers Clark in the frontier Indian wars. The relative, who gave me all of the information about this figure from the past, gave me a great way to talk about a figure from history who would have known about all of the events and characters and could speak with authority about them.

DEMOCRATIC CONNECTIONS

Citizenship education is predicated on the idea of active participants who make effective decisions for themselves and others that will perpetuate democratic society. Teachers capture the imagination of students and help students want to explore and experience social studies. Students start making decisions early in their school career and work toward making decisions that will benefit civil society (Alleman, Knighton, & Brophy, 2007). Students practice decision-making skills at school and learn to make good decisions in their homes. Students tackle real problems and make decisions to solve them. Shirley Engle championed decision-making in the social studies curriculum as the focal point of citizenship education (Gallavan, 2003). These citizens endeavor to make good choices through decision-making in the present and in the future. Students who encounter issue-centered social studies learn to recognize issues and make decisions in political life. Students learn about issue-centered social studies through engaging citizenship and making connections to the past (Chilcoat & Ligon, 2000). As students become acquainted with and begin examining issues, they meet people who lived through those issues and had views about those issues. The students engage in decision-making just as people from the past engaged in decision-making. Students see and interact with people who have experiences in democratic citizenship and use the experiences of first-person characters to help them practice citizenship skills.

CONTROVERSIAL ISSUES

First-person presentations are great ways to help students deal with controversial issues because the students get opportunities to examine issues from the past. The issue needs to have meaning for the students; that is, the issue needs to be an issue the students have confronted, will confront, or have a concern about at this time. The issue has meaning to society in that it represents the view of a majority or minority of the people. There is considerable interest in the issue, and it impacts the well-being of a group of people. The issue has endured across time, and at different periods of time the issue reappeared as a concern of society. Controversial issues have:

- Meaning to students
- Meaning to society
- Endured across time
- Been faced by people in other places

People in other places may also be faced with this issue. This may be replicated in other parts of a community, other parts of a state, within a nation, or around the world. For example, Joseph Neef, an educator in Robert Owen's utopian community of New Harmony, provided high-quality educational opportunities for both males and females. This issue certainly resonates to one-half of the students because they want opportunities for themselves, future spouses, future children, and grandchildren. Joseph Neef can talk about how important equal education was to the people in Owen's New Harmony. Since it was a utopian group, it was important to help all people become well educated because they would make the decisions for the community. Set within the context of gender equity, students look at this question both in the present and across time. The issue has resonance to society. For example, in the past some families educated women in colonial America and others did not; college degrees and graduate programs have become available to women in the past few generations. The lingering interest of how best to educate boys and how to encourage girls in math and science illustrates the continuing interest in this issue over time. After

Joseph Neef talks about education at New Harmony, the teacher can follow the presentation by helping students find how this is still an issue today not only for American women but for women in the Middle East and in Africa as well.

MULTIPLE PERSPECTIVES

In a first-person presentation the character interacts with the audience as opposed to a wax dummy in an amusement park attraction that performs regardless of the number of people viewing it. Although you may want to investigate multiple perspectives, a first-person character can show only one perspective—that of the character being portrayed. For example, after the teacher assumed and sustained the role of an Amish man for about ten minutes, he asked the students to contrast the character to their lives. In small groups the students compared and contrasted the life of the Amish man to their life with the use of a common Venn diagram. In order to explore three different perspectives, the students asked this character questions that compared him to a character they had recently met. For example, the students asked questions that compared the Amish man to a Shaker man, both of whom they met in their unit on diversity of thought. The students asked, "How do you use technology and why?" The students also provided their response to this question so they displayed all three views in vertical columns that displayed their answers. For a fourth perspective, students interviewed two characters, the characters questioned each other, and both characters questioned the students. For example, a woman who represented a daughter who had left the Amish community joined the Amish man. The students asked the Amish man, "What keeps you in the Amish community?" The students asked the young woman, "Why did you decide to leave the Amish?" The Amish man asked the students, "How will you survive without a close-knit community?" The Amish woman asked the students, "What will you expect to be after you graduate?" The Amish man asked the young woman, "Don't you love your family?" The young woman asked the Amish man, "Why can't I know more about the world by attending high school?" By working with multiple perspectives in first-person presentations, the students compared their lives to the lives of others, and they learned about perspectives different from their own. By using first-person characters, teachers can help students see multiple perspectives:

- The perspective of the character
- Contrast the perspective of the character to the perspective of the students
- Contrast the perspective of the character to the perspective of a different character the students have met in the past
- Contrast the perspective of the character to the perspective of another character and the perspective of the student to interact with both characters

Teachers helped students learn about the experiences of others from different times or places. Students learned to seek social justice when they met a pioneer of 1825 from central Indiana. The event he recounted was the series of murders on Fall Creek where white men murdered a group of Indians. The students used the primary sources of the time to recreate the events surrounding the trial with the first-person presenter. They passed a moral judgment as to the guilt of the men and used the words of the judge in sentencing the men. It was the first time in American history that a white man was found guilty of murdering an Indian, and he was hanged for it.

CREATING FIRST-PERSON PRESENTATIONS

To create a first-person presentation requires a lot of thought about the structure and content of the presentation. When you begin your presentation, the audience can pretty much guess that your character will be successful, but the difficulties along the way, the obstacles, and the struggles present the tension for your program that will keep the audience on the edge of their seats. Early in the process of constructing your character, you will wish to consider

Table 1.1. First-person Presentation Checklist

Completed	Preparation	Development	Criteria	Details
	Idea			
		Identity/Perspective		
	Story			
		Beginning		
			Artifacts/AV/Photos	
			Time	Idea that defines the time
				Idea that transcends the time
			Place	
		Middle		
			Stories that reflect upon your character	
			Stories about friends that reflect upon their character	
			Connections to the common man	
			Content accuracy	
			Alternative interpretation	
			Disclaimer of myths or legends	
		End		

whether you wish to speak for someone who is famous or if you want
to select a less well-known character. You may start with an idea,
such as the idea of how you could teach about an entrepreneur. Let
us select the example of Colonel Eli Lilly. He needs to have both an
identity and a perspective. He comes to Indianapolis after the Civil
War and starts a business manufacturing medicines in a simple two-
story brick building on the south side of Indianapolis.

Our character needs a story that tells about his life. Eli Lilly's
story parallels that of many other veterans who left their homes for
the Civil War, found their way into other locations, and looked for
work or an opportunity after the war. Before describing the person's
birth and early childhood, many biographies start with the parents
or even the grandparents of the person being written about. Most
first-person presentations do not have that much time, and the
audience expects the character to jump right into the action. The
beginning of the presentation needs to start with a quick explosion
of interesting content and action. For Eli Lilly, the prospect of
ending the Civil War and a new beginning as a civilian gives just
that sort of tension that makes the listener want to find out what
happens next.

You need to determine the props, historic clothing, audiovisu-
als, maps, or photographs that will help you tell your story and ori-
ent your audience to your story. For Eli Lilly, I select a frock coat
and top hat, photos of Eli in Civil War uniform, and photos of his
company on McCarty Street. The frock coat and top hat identify
him as a prosperous member of the community. The Civil War
picture sets him in a context and reveals some of his past experiences. The photo of the business shows the extent of his present
accomplishments.

Toward the beginning of the program I want to define the time
as being during the 1880s. I share the fact that this is an election
year and that I always vote for the Grand Army of the Republic can-
didate; I will therefore be voting for Benjamin Harrison as president
of the United States. I also want to talk about an idea that tran-
scends the time and has application to today, so I elect to talk about
veterans' groups asking for health care for wounded or enfeebled
veterans. It is also important to set the stage of the presentation by

explaining the place that will help the students to understand that it is relatively close to where they live. For Col. Eli Lilly, Pearl Street on the south side of Indianapolis was in the warehouse district that was close to the railroad station, hotels of a variety of classes, and the stockyards.

In the middle of the first-person presentation is a good opportunity to develop the character of the individual by telling stories about his or her life. On Sundays after church, Eli drove around the outskirts of town to find herbs he suspected might prove beneficial (Kahn, 1989). Further, stories about their friends that impact the character of the individual are important to add so that it does not sound like the person is always talking about how great he is. Col. Eli Lilly gave an impoverished boy $2.50, enabling him to return to his home in Texas (Kahn, 1989). The character needs to establish connections to the common man either as a common man himself or herself or through acts that show how he or she relates to the common man. Otherwise, the character will seem to be made out of marble and become a larger-than-life statue rather than a human being. For example, within walking distance from Lilly's business were heavily foreign ethnic neighborhoods, meatpacking plants, milling establishments, a large Jewish population, the farmers' market, the major retail district, and the statehouse. For any first-person presentation content accuracy requires a high standard of excellence, and alternative interpretations can be introduced into the first-person presentation. On the one hand, the medicines that Col. Eli Lilly produced were purer than those of his competitors and that gave him an edge over the competition. On the other hand, Col. Eli Lilly was making what would today be called patent medicines rather than the highly regulated and monitored pharmaceuticals required by modern industry standards. It is also important to dispel myths, legends, or misconceptions that the audience members hold. One common myth is that Col. Eli Lilly never produced patent medicines, yet one of the first pieces of equipment the Colonel purchased was an alcohol still. To conclude the first-person presentation, one must give the students a task to complete based on the life of the character. For Col. Eli Lilly, you might ask the students if they think the Colonel could have been successful in his business at this time if he never put alcohol in his medicines. The students will have lots of questions, and when they get into groups to answer this question they will have much to talk about with their partners.

FIRST-PERSON PRESENTATION IN AN EDUCATIONAL CONTEXT

The purpose of using first-person presentations in an educational context is to help the students learn knowledge, skills, and attributes. It looks deceptively easy when you meet a ranger in the National Park Service or an interpreter at Conner Prairie. You might even have an old hat that will help you set the stage, but beware

Table 1.2. First-person Presentation Set in an Educational Context Checklist

Completed	Criteria	Guiding Questions
_____	Concept	
_____	Objective	
_____	Standard	
_____	Assessment	
_____		What are the students going to do?
_____	Key moment	
_____	Controversial issue	
_____	Research background	
_____		What primary sources will you use?
_____		What secondary sources will you use?
_____		What original artwork or photographs will you use from that time to determine clothing?
_____		What slang will you use or avoid?
_____	Logistics	
_____		Where do you want the students located?
_____		How will you enter or exit the room?
_____	Rehearsal	

because as cool as that old hat may be, it gives you only about ten seconds before the audience expects you to do something with it. You had better have something great to say, and in order to have something to say requires that you have thought about your teaching. You will need to focus on a concept, an idea that is central to your lesson that you want your students to learn. In a first-person historical presentation of Jean Maurice, a French fur trader in the Wabash Valley prior to 1750, the concept is that of mutually beneficial trade between the Indians and the French.

In addition to a concept, it is important to have an objective because it helps to define what the students do as a result of this experience. In this case the students create a map of the French posts and portages in the Ohio River Valley. This objective should match a standard. The National Council for the Social Studies standard of "Production, Consumption, and Distribution" certainly fits as does "People, Places, and Environments." At the same time you create the objective, you need to construct a matching assessment. It is easy to see from the objective that the assessment in this lesson requires students to create a map of rivers in the Ohio Valley, to identify French posts located next to major Indian villages, and to illustrate the portages between the rivers that the French used for transportation routes. Students illustrate what they have learned through participation in the first-person presentation when they demonstrate their learning by successfully accomplishing the objective and assessment.

Always try to find the key moment in history, and for Jean Maurice it was gathering with the Indians to trade and take the furs to Québec. That was the high point of his year when all of the work he did paid off politically, economically, and socially. Try to find a controversial issue, which for Jean Maurice was the control of the Indian trade. Will the Indians trade with him, or will they trade with the English who seem to be entering land that belongs to France? The interaction of at least three desires can play out here, illustrating the wants of the Indians, French, and English. Teachers find the key moment and controversial issues through research. It is important to research the background of the time and the character using both primary and secondary sources. A primary source is one that was created by the people who witnessed the events at the time the events occurred. A book that contains multiple French colonial primary sources is *Travel accounts of Indiana 1679–1961* (McCord, 1970). These sources are translated from the original French and are easy to read in the typed edition. A secondary source is written after the fact by analyzing the primary sources and interpreting the events. Barnhart and Riker's (1971) book *Indiana to 1816* is a secondary source book that contains information about colonial New France. Since there are no photographs from this time, the best way to determine clothing is to look at original art work from the time (Johnson, Forbes, & Delaney, 1982). Slang, both what you say and what you do not say, is important. This is an important part of the research, and it is a subtle way to help students learn about the time in question. Maurice referred to those people in the fur trade who wintered in Quebec as "pork eaters," but he would never have said, "Back in the day" since that phrase is just a couple decades old.

Actors think about how they will organize space around themselves and between other people. For logistics think about how you are going to greet the students. Where will you be? Will you come into the classroom? Do you need someone to watch your classroom until you arrive? Where do you want the students? What do you want them to do? How will you end the presentation? How will you exit the room? Using space to help students learn about the character is important; it tells the students if the character is approachable, intimate, or socially superior. For Maurice, I usually met the students in character as they came into the room and started the day with them. After starting in character it was easy to progress to other activities either still in character or out of character.

Finally, consider the importance of rehearsals; since this is something new, practice is required. Talk to the mirror, call your parents or grandparent—they want to hear from you, talk to your partner, talk to the dog, talk to your friends, and talk to your friend's dog. Think about what you will do with your hands, how you will move your body, and what your facial expressions will be. Think about what you will say, how you will use your voice, what will be the pace and inflection of your voice, and how you will project the dynamics of your voice. With this kind of planning and forethought, you will become very polished and proficient at giving first-person historical presentations.

All teachers instruct from their personality and their educational philosophy. Who you are defines which characters you can easily portray, but who you are not also defines the roles you can easily play. I was once criticized for not having women's clothing and thus not providing a good model for the girls in my class. While I understand the thought, in practice that did not seem like a really good idea; the students would never have believed that I was a woman. It would have been so distracting that it would have taken away from the stories, ideas, and discussion I was trying to spark. That idea was of dubious value for the effort required.

I wanted to bring different perspectives into the classroom, and to do that required multiple voices. To talk about Little Turtle and Tecumseh, I thought it best to have my character have a French trader for a father and to be a warrior. With my heavy beard and really pale skin it was still a bit of a stretch, but as time has progressed and gravity descends upon me I now look more like a village elder. No one would ever believe that I am black, Asian, or even from India. While makeup is possible in the world of theater, pragmatic teachers cannot afford the time that makeup requires. I can easily take the role of a slave owner, slave catcher, or Underground Railroad conductor, and I can make all of these roles come to life instantly. Further, I once knew a teacher who said her audience would never confuse her with Cleopatra, the most beautiful woman of the ancient world, so she elected to become a serving woman in Cleopatra's court. That way she did not need to compete with Elizabeth Taylor.

The rest of this book will look at a variety of perspectives and techniques for using first-person presentations in a variety of grade levels from second to eighth grades. There is at least one successful example for each grade level mentioned in this book. Each of the teachers described has been successful with this technique, continues to develop new characters, and reuses characters that have been successful in the past. These teachers are always experimenting, testing, and challenging themselves with something new to help their students become excited about the social studies content, skills, and attributes in the curriculum. None of these teachers use this method every day or even every week, but they do use a variety of methods to keep their students on the edge of their seats.

THOUGHT QUESTIONS

1. How will a teacher acquire the background knowledge needed to conduct these types of programs?
2. What is the difference between entertainment and education? Is a first-person presentation one or the other?
3. What relative could you portray in a first-person historical presentation?

REFERENCES

Alleman, J., Knighton, B., & Brophy, J. (2007). Social studies: Incorporating all children using community and cultural universals as the centerpiece. *Journal of Learning Disabilities, 40*(2), 166–173.

Barnhart, J. D., & Riker, L. D. (1971). *Indiana to 1816: The colonial period*. Indianapolis, IN: Indiana Historical Bureau and Indiana Historical Society.

Chilcoat, G. W., & Ligon, J. A. (2000). Issues-centered instruction in the elementary social studies classroom. *Theory and Research in Social Education, 28*(2), 220–272.

Gallavan, N. P. (2003). Decision making, self-efficacy, and the place of career. *Social Studies, 94*(1), 15–19.

Johnson, M. M., Forbes, J., & Delaney, K. (1982). *Historic colonial French dress: A guide to recreating North American French clothing*. West Lafayette, IN: Ouabache Press.

Kahn, E. J. (1989). *All in a century: The first 100 years of Eli Lilly and Company*. Indianapolis, IN: Eli Lilly and Company.

McCord, S. S. (1970). *Travel accounts of Indiana 1679–1961: A collection of observations by wayfaring foreigners, itinerants, and peripatetic Hoosiers*. Indiana Historical Collections XLVII. Indianapolis, IN: Indiana Historical Bureau.

Chapter Two

─────────────○─────────────

Second Grade
Presidents' Day[1]

THE SECOND-GRADE STUDENTS OF All Saints School perform first-person historical presentations using all the presidents of the United States as their characters. They present a one-minute overview of the president's life in first-person characterization including costumes. They do this in connection with Presidents' Day; the students study the American presidency from the time they return to school after New Year's Day until Presidents' Day. They perform on stage and in front of an assemblage of parents, grandparents, friends, and media representatives. After doing extensive research the students use the results to interpret their specific president in front of a public audience; the students compile a speech and deliver their presentations about their presidents. Winebrenner (1992) as well as Cruz and Murthy (2006) suggest that students create first-person presentations as a way to study social studies.

RATIONALE

Using Drama to Learn Social Studies

"In order to feel part of the world around us, we need a basic tap root—a root that goes deep into the shared experiences of our culture" (Webb, Meckstroth, & Tolan, 1982, p. 177; Brewer, 2006). The teachers use drama to help the students share what they have

15

learned with the audience. Students tap into their community
when they realize that their parents, teachers, and the audience
all want them to be successful. These community members ask
students to demonstrate historical thinking skills through drama.
Teachers have found drama to be an effective way to teach social
studies with high levels of student participation (Fines & Verrie,
1974; Morris, 1998, 2003; Taylor, 1998). When students use
drama in social studies, they demonstrate increased evidence of
thinking skills (Fink, 2001; Goalen & Hendy, 1993). The students
explore the presidents by using drama as a method of learning social
studies. They take on roles, discuss decisions, and establish context
in their characters. Students must establish which items are most
important when they tell their story. When students demonstrate
thinking skills, they practice social studies that they can use for the
rest of their life. As students work with their parents they learn to
think; they use drama to explore their characters more fully; and the
students gain confidence by successfully presenting their characters before a public audience.

Parents as Teachers

Parents continue to make contributions to their child's education
just as they have guided their child's education up to this point.
The teachers are providing an opportunity for the parent to work in
tandem with the school. "Research results indicate that teaching in
the home includes modeling, direct instruction, coaching, simulation, making comparison, interactive play, supervision, and indirect
instruction through setting predisposition" (Sunal, 1991). Parents
help the students with this project; the parents work with students
by reading to them and helping them record their thoughts. The
parents set up an expectation and a pattern of supporting their child
in successful school activities. Eight- and nine-year-olds exhibit
developmental thinking when they recognize the likelihood of conflicts and the concept of rulers (Williams, 2005; Wymer & Farquar,
1991). The students must think about leaders: what makes a good
leader and how they would act if they were leaders. The second-
grade students explore what presidents have done for the country

and how those experiences include conflict between groups and individuals. While all presidents were not equally strong leaders, each of them contributed to the democratic process.

PROCEDURES

Conducting the Research

Maker (1982) describes inquiry models where students interpret data. Students must then discriminate between salient and irrelevant data to construct their presentations. Students pick a president by lottery, research and write about their president, and then present information about them in the first person. The teachers included some first ladies also who follow their husband's presentation in chronological order. These ladies include the wives of the two presidents with February birthdays, George Washington and Abraham Lincoln, plus the current first lady. These students find out much more about the American presidency during Presidents' Day than coloring black line masters or a cluster of cherries and a hatchet or a stovepipe hat for the birthdays of Washington and Lincoln. Both peers and community evaluate how students demonstrate and use their knowledge because they perform in a public arena to demonstrate their understanding of their president.

Teachers provide guiding questions to help students focus on the major achievements and highlights of their president's life:

1. What important event happened during your term of office?
2. Why do we remember you as an important president?

   a. Contributions to country
   b. Conflict between groups and individuals

3. What are some interesting things about yourself, such as childhood, family, or hobbies?

Teachers also ask parents to read books with their child, discuss what their child found out, and orally ask their children to answer the questions before the child starts to write the report. The teachers suggest that dates and place names do not have meaning for this age child, and students should minimize their use in the report. Teachers send letters home at the beginning of the project and periodically thereafter describing the project, its goals, and how to help the students achieve the goals of the project. Teachers encourage parents to learn and work with their children on this project, and parents guide and encourage students to start searching for and interpreting information. Students benefit by observing their parent learning and knowing that they help adults learn about the topic, too. In the program, students disseminate knowledge that is unfamiliar to many adults, and the cumulative effect is that the project is educational for adults as well.

Students come to school excited about what they have recently learned while searching for information about their president, and they naturally want to share that knowledge. Teachers build upon the students' excitement in sharing information while encouraging them to learn more that they can disseminate later in their presentations. Class begins every morning with the new facts that the students have learned about their president and reports from the previous evening's activities. The teachers use class time to help the students find more books, write the report in their own words, and work on the mechanics of writing. Preparation for this program is included in every part of the day; for example, in reading groups the students evaluate the volume of their reading voices in preparation for public speaking. Students build their possible speech by gathering new information each evening, and this stack of notes grows until the student narrows it down into their speech.

Getting Ready for the Presentation

In second grade, students focus on communities moving from home and school into the greater community, and the students learn about the three branches of government. The students and the teachers each write a Bill of Rights; the teachers and the students then compare and compromise until they have a Bill of Rights for the grade level. Students learn how the legislature makes decisions, they learn about leaders, and they learn about the qualities of a good leader. Students follow this preparation with individual writing, "If I were president . . ." In this essay they discuss how they would be a good leader and how they would exercise power. All of these experiences culminate when the students study the presidents. In this essay the teachers ask the student to evaluate information and ideas and make ethical decisions.

The students script their characters and perform their presentations for one another in the classroom and on the stage. Students practice using the microphone on two days, and they practice both the speech and the program procedures. Students need to feel comfortable and confident that they know their material. Students also need to know how they will come in, how they will find their seat, when they go to the podium, and how to sit without creating distractions. Since this is their first time to make a speech or to use a microphone, students get instructions on how to stand and how to speak so that all can hear and see.

Students go to great lengths to find artifacts and costuming that are appropriate for their characterization. For example, FDR rolled in seated in an antique wheel chair, and Ike wore his World War II uniform. Many students wear campaign buttons for their character; for example, Benjamin Harrison's button said, "He wears his grandfather's hat!" Students must do additional research to find out what people wore in that time period and what things relate to their person or characterize them best. Students must find out about politics and elections to find what campaign slogans and issues went on the political buttons. Even the cosmetic part of the project provides opportunities for students to learn more about their character.

Assessment

On the day after Presidents' Day the students are ready, and they arrive in costume. The teacher gives a brief welcome before the students enter the auditorium to the music, "Hail to the Chief." The students put all of their preparation to work as they present flawlessly. The students do their one-minute characterization while TV cameras arrive to film them, and camera flashes go off all around them. One by one as their teacher calls their real name, the students give their first-person presentations before a full gym. The presentations include two or three parts:

1. Introduction of the character
2. Context of the character including work and job; historical significance

   a. Conflict between groups or individuals

3. An amusing story about their president is optional

Students report on their president's major achievements and important highlights. There is an opportunity for a presidential photo shoot; it is the only opportunity for the audience to get a picture of all the presidents at one time. The students adjourn to a light cake-and-punch reception where they meet their parents and visitors.

Each member of the crowd evaluates the student's performance before a public audience; the students display their competency prominently before the adults of the community. It is obvious to all that the teachers have worked hard to insure that each of these students demonstrates competency to stand before a crowd and present their story successfully. Each student knows that they have succeeded in learning how leaders help government operate; if they have any doubt as to the quality of their presentation, they can watch the VCR tape of their performance. The community rarely calls upon second-grade students to read, write, and speak in public on a specific topic where their teachers, parents, and friends witness their success. The students discover that they can speak before an audience, and they use this successful experience to give them confidence for future challenges. When students interpret their presidents, they use content described in one or more of the ten National Council for the Social Studies standards (NCSS, 1994) [see appendix II]. Concepts and generalizations cluster under these standards. Students apply content to their presidents while meeting standards that help them understand their world. The standards with the most connections include:

I. Culture
II. Time, Continuity, and Change
III. People, Places, and Environments
V. Individuals, Groups, and Institutions

For example, the student can interpret the life of a president as a leader of a democracy and explore the national social studies standard "Power, Authority, and Governance." Students tackle a variety of subjects in their presentations and as each student presents a minute, the audience learns about multiple standards. Students use content from anthropology, geography, history, and sociology to make their presentations informative.

The community members learn information from the first-person presentations that they did not previously know. The community has a common experience because each student in the older grades did this when they were in second grade. The community members not only enjoy seeing the person talk, but the community members also enjoy their tradition of celebrating Presidents' Day in this special way. The community members also celebrate the accomplishments of the second-grade students. Teachers, students, and community members appreciate the parental support and the drama work of the students.

EXAMPLE

When her teacher calls her name, Cece walks to the podium, checks her notes, and speaks to the audience with the microphone. She wears a black frock coat and trousers, white shirt, and black tie. She stands poised without fear, with neither a tremble in her hand nor a waver in her voice as she gives her speech.

> Hi! My name is William Henry Harrison, and I was the ninth president to be elected. I was sixty-seven years old and the oldest president before Ronald Reagan. My inaugural speech was two hours long making it the longest in history. I gave it on a cold,

rainy day causing me to catch a cold that became pneumonia. A month later I died making me the first president to die in office. This is the shortest term a president has served. I came from a family of great politicians. My father signed the Declaration of Independence, and my grandson became the twenty-third president, Benjamin Harrison.

She remains in character and while she is sometimes omniscient, she only uses this characteristic to interpret and compare her character to other presidents. She also makes connections for the audience to help them place her character in history when she discusses the significance of the family members.

CONCLUSIONS

In an effort to help all of the students in the school attain high levels of achievement, students take on an acceleration project requiring them to work with content usually reserved for eighth-grade students. Students work with biography and first-person historic presentation. Acceleration projects require students to work with content in-depth (Feldhusen, VanTassel-Baska, & Seeley 1989). The depth of information occurs when students work with their families to conduct research on their president and then create a presentation describing their life. The communication and presentation skills which students use allow them to present the information they have learned to others. Students working with parents and teachers learn the process of research in a structured formula that allows them to be successful.

Teachers get an opportunity to share the accomplishments of the second-grade students with the community. Teachers need multiple opportunities to help students connect with the community by performing their competency in a public forum. Teachers help the students realize that the public views them as competent. Community members need to realize that the schools succeed in helping young people grow and develop. Teachers are successful in preparing students to share information with the method called acting through drama.

Students get to learn and share information about the presidency, and they also learn to convey information while working with an audience. Students work with their parents to gather information in support of what they are learning in school. Students then take pleasure in performing before their parents, relatives, and friends of the family. Students get to work with their parents as well as use drama to communicate what they have learned with the audience. Students demonstrate research skills and share this research through elaborate communication.

THOUGHT QUESTIONS

1. What experiences with social history could compliment this experience?
2. How can this expenditure of time be justified with the pressure to achieve reading and writing expectations?
3. Could students who did not have an involved parent be successful with this project?

NOTE

1. Morris, R. V. (2002). Presidents' Day in second grade with first-person presentation. *Gifted Child Today*, 25(4), 26–29, 64. Reprinted with the permission of Prufrock Press Inc. (http://www.prufrock.com).

REFERENCES

Brewer, E. A. (2006). Keep social studies in the elementary school. *Childhood Education*, 82(5), 296–298.

Cruz, B. C., & Murthy, S. A. (2006). Breathing life into history: Using role-playing to engage students. *Social Studies and the Young Learner*, 19(1), 4–8.

Feldhusen, J., VanTassel-Baska, J., & Seeley, K. (1989). *Excellence in educating the gifted*. Denver, CO: Love.

Fines, J., & Verrie, R. (1974). *The drama of history: An experiment in cooperative teaching*. London: New University Education.

Fink, L. (2001). New tidings for history education, or lessons we should have learned by now. *History Teachers, 34*(2), 235–242.

Goalen, P., & Hendy, L. (1993). 'It's not just fun, it works!' Developing children's historical thinking through drama. *Curriculum Journal, 4*(3), 363–384.

Maker, J. C. (1982). *Teaching models in education of the gifted*. Rockville, MD: Aspen Systems.

Morris, R. V. (2003). The nation's capital and first graders: Role playing a trip to Washington, D.C. *Social Studies, 94*(6), 265–269.

———. (1998). Common threads: How to translate best practice into teaching. *Journal of Social Studies Research, 22*(2), 11–18.

National Council for the Social Studies. (1994). *Expectations of excellence: Curriculum standards for social studies*. Washington, D.C.: Author.

Sunal, C. S. (1991). The influence of the home on social studies. In J. P. Shaver (Ed.), *Handbook of research on social studies teaching and learning* (pp. 290–299). New York: Macmillan.

Taylor, P. (1998). *Redcoats and patriots: Reflective practice in drama and social studies*. Portsmouth, NH: Heinemann.

Webb, J. T., Meckstroth, E. A., & Tolan, S. S. (1982). *Guiding the gifted child*. Columbus, OH: Ohio Psychology.

Williams, D. (2005). A dream we all can share: How parents can teach kids that all history counts. *Teaching Tolerance, 27*, 18–19.

Winebrenner, S. (1992). *Teaching gifted kids in the regular classroom*. Minneapolis, MN: Free Spirit.

Wymer, N. B., & Farquar, E. (1991). Cognitive, emotional, and social development: Early childhood social studies. In J. P. Shaver (Ed.), *Handbook of research on social studies teaching and learning* (pp. 109–120). New York: Macmillan.

Chapter Three

───────────────○───────────────

Third Grade at
Simmons School[1]

THE THIRD-GRADE STUDENTS at Hope Elementary School in Hope, Indiana, step out of their modern school building and walk down a path to Simmons Elementary School, a one-room brick schoolhouse where they experience a day of school as it might have been lived a century ago.[2] By studying life at the turn of the twentieth century, students learn a little about what life was like when their great grandparents or earlier residents of the community went to school. For this special day, teachers are prepared to act as third-grade grammar school instructors from a century ago, with appropriate lessons and materials.[3] They also talk about the social history of a century ago, relating anecdotes from that era, engaging their students with interesting social studies content throughout the day (Clark, 2000; Hahn, 1998). Students also choose a role, such as the "mischievous child with a sprained ankle," and interpret the part throughout the events of the day, which is always one to be remembered.

ENGAGING IN THE DRAMA OF HISTORY

Of course young students use the National Council for the Social Studies standards (1994) [see appendix II] when they learn about history by experiencing a small segment of time in great detail including:

II. Time, Continuity, and Change
III. People, Places, and Environments
V. Individuals, Groups, and Institutions

Students can learn content and skills by taking on roles, interpreting characters, making decisions in a simulated environment, and then evaluating the effect of their actions (Catterall, 2007; Downey & Levstik, 1991; Edinger, 2005; Fines & Verrier, 1974; Goalen & Hendy, 1993; Kelin, 2002; Morris & Welch, 2000; Tanner, 2001; Wilson, 2002). Through the process of dramatizing everyday experiences and notable events from their community's past, students learn how history confronts each generation with interesting experiences and challenges. Students then begin to see how history applies to their lives. Students learn content and skills in situations where they engage in dramatic play by taking roles and interpreting characters. "Role-playing is an important part, of games and simulations . . . The purpose . . . is to bring out the dramatic quality of a situation, as in the re-creation of a historical setting such as a mock trial or a constitutional convention" (Clegg, 1991). With the use of some creative props and some drama, history can come alive for third graders.

PREPARATION

Barb Johnson, a third-grade teacher, writes a letter to parents about the day the class will spend in a one-room schoolhouse. She states the purpose of the event: "Students act as though they are students living one hundred years ago. We will pretend to go back in time and will attempt to live life as people did then." Before beginning the role-playing, the students spend a week examining how their community has changed and grown over the last one hundred years, as well as briefly looking at how American public education has changed. They talk about the people in the community who attended the school. They learn that the Simmons Elementary School building was once used in the Bartholomew County school district, but four miles away. They also learn how high school students helped the community to document, move, and preserve the schoolhouse.

On a timeline, students place images of inventions from the eighteenth and nineteenth century. Mrs. Johnson helps the students imagine what technology would have been available to people in 1900. For example, Mrs. Johnson has the students compare dates and asks if they would have had phonographs in 1900, the time of the schoolhouse simulation. Students try to figure out what the phonograph is because most of the students do not know about record players; however, one of the students, Zach, tells them about both seeing and using a record player. She also asks what the sources of light and heat were in the old school. The answer is: oil lamps and a wood- or coal-burning stove. She asks questions, such as, "Which do you think would be easier to use: coal or wood?" Students respond with their own questions like "Do we have to carry wood when we visit the old school?" The answer is "No, the coal is delivered by a truck, but you must take turns filling the coal shuttle and stoking the stove." Mrs. Johnson asks students to note how many years ago their town got electricity and to evaluate how that technology changed their town.

BACKGROUND READINGS

Literature and primary historical sources are important resources in this third-grade class. Mrs. Johnson reads aloud from *The World of the Little House* (Collins & Eriksson, 1996). The author, Laura Wilder, and her husband both attended a one-room school; later Wilder served as a teacher in a one-room school. Mrs. Johnson reads a bit from the book then relates it to the Simmons Elementary School. After she talks about teachers earning twelve dollars per month, she then asks, "Why was that small salary acceptable in that time?" Ashley responds, "Money was worth a lot then." Mrs. Johnson adds, "And many things did not cost as much then." After making this economic comparison, Mrs. Johnson has the students examine the moral aspects of education a century ago. The *New England Primer* (1805), from which many students learned the alphabet, had entries with moral lessons; for example, for the Letter F: "The idle Fool is whipped at school," and references to Bible verses for the letter A: "In Adam's fall, we sinned all." Mrs. Johnson also used primary sources of rules and teacher contracts from the Simmons School District.

MONDAY MORNING IN 1900

On the day of the simulation, Mrs. Johnson opens the old school before the students arrive. She checks that there are slates and slate pencils at each desk. She brings water and ice from the modern school. She checks the cabinets for recess games, pulls out the tin drinking cups, and locates the *McGuffey's Eclectic Spelling Book* (1879) for the third grade. There is a quotation from the book of Proverbs in the Bible written on the chalkboard. She is ready for the day.

Students come dressed in costumes appropriate for school children at the turn of the century. Girls wear long skirts or dresses; some have bonnets on their heads. Boys wear knickers or sweatpants rolled up to below the knee; long white or dark socks; and maybe suspenders. When the school bell rings, the students enter from out of the spring drizzle. They place their lunches and hats in the small cloakroom.

Mrs. Johnson splits the class into three groups: students who pretend to be younger sit in the front of the classroom; those pretending to be in the middle level sit in the middle of the classroom; those pretending to be older sit in the back of the room. The students understand that there are many different grades mixed into their one-room school. Mrs. Johnson tries to capture the imagination of the students by helping them pretend that they are living in another time. Once they take their seats, Mrs. Johnson gives a brief overview of the day; then asks the students to shut their eyes as she counts backward from three to zero. When they open their eyes, the students have been transported back in time one hundred years.

Mrs. Johnson provides the students with an introductory ritual to help the students realize that they are starting the historic school day. These include call and response, oral introduction, group singing, and physical gestures. "Good morning, boys and girls," says Mrs. Johnson. The students respond, "Good morning, Mrs. Johnson." She asks the children to stand and teaches the good morning song, in which they sing, "Good morning to you; Good morning to you," before they bow or curtsy. Before calling the roll, Mrs. Johnson delivers a brief first-person monologue about discipline, her expectations, and the behavior that their fathers demand of them. The fathers in the patriarchal home lives of that time would have set the tone for school. Mrs. Johnson is able to give additional information through first-person historical presentation.

Mrs. Johnson scoured old local newspaper articles for stories about school-aged children from long ago that she includes in the reenactment. She calls each child by name and has comments to make to each student as he or she stands at attention. She helps them get into their roles by "admonishing" certain individuals for fictitious "shortcomings in their conduct" that had "occurred the previous day." One mischief maker is still limping from trying to "fly off the barn roof," one "played in the creek on the way to school," and another had "stayed home to plow." Even yesterday's assistant is admonished for "poor cleaning of the classroom." Mrs. Johnson asks for a new assistant, and all the students raise their hands. By this time it is easy to see that the students are completely committed to the historical reenactment. She asks that students who ride horses to school "tie them up so they will not get away. Also, do not throw rocks at the neighbors' cows." Of course, when one student comes in late, the teacher "chastises him for being tardy." Mrs. Johnson did not just make up a series of humorous stories to amuse the students. The stories that did not come from the newspaper came from oral history interviews done with former students at the school. This information provided rich human detail verified by sources.

RABBIT STEW

Mrs. Johnson is not all severity and discipline. She also had stories from oral history and newspapers that reflected positively on the students and their families. She passes out compliments liberally; for example, she mentions the dress one girl's ma recently made for her. She thanks various students for "bringing a rabbit for my stew," "fixing a spoke on my wagon so that I could go to the Teachers' Institute," "giving me some homemade jam and butter," and for "offering an invitation for Sunday dinner." Many of the compliments Mrs. Johnson offered were for gifts or food or acts of kindness. These kind acts reflected well on the memories that people share about life in a small town. The memories also reflect on an agricultural economy that still provided many goods and services through barter and trade.

Mrs. Johnson also provides news about socials such as the upcoming quilting bee. The "box social" causes quite a stir: the girls present box lunches, and the boys save their pennies to bid on the boxes. A story is told that last year a student bid on the wrong lunch. The teacher asks some students to stay after school to clean the chimneys and others to sweep the floor and wash the chalkboards before the box social. Mrs. Johnson makes a great deal of mentioning the work done in the community, and one student offers to provide the paint and to paint the schoolhouse trim. She offers money to any student who offers to plow the teacher's garden and set in the tomato plants, while noting that some children ought to stay home and chop up tree limbs that fell in the recent storm. She is skeptical about setting up an old bushel basket in the back of the school so that students can throw a ball through it, but she finally grants permission for students to try out this "new game"—basketball. She also advises a folk remedy to a student's brother who "let the ax slip and cut his leg."

Students raise their hands to speak. One student tells about a trip to Columbus, Indiana, to see a show in a theater. That community had electric streetlights! Another student asks if she can lead the pledge to the flag, and students then recite an early version lacking the phrase "under God." Finally, the teacher reminds the students of the posture they should exhibit in their seats during the day's lessons.

LESSONS: BACK TO BASICS

The lessons involve three groups of scholars. The "younger" students rise and read their lessons from *McGuffey's Eclectic Spelling Book* at the recitation benches. Reading groups stand to sing the vowel letters and sounds. The "middle" students work on arithmetic at the front board and at their desk on slates. The "upper-level" students write their names with pen and ink on tablets. Mrs. Johnson teaches all of them how to use ink pens and inkwells. Then students rotate groups; throughout the day they get to belong to each of the three groups.

The students come together as a whole class for the next lessons. First, the students have a "spell down," then they learn directions and geography by facing in the appropriate direction and chanting a verse:

East is Ohio's fertile land
North to the tract called Michigan
West Illinois and South the stream
Of the Ohio may be seen

Students also chant their multiplication tables; today they work on multiples of five. Next, Mrs. Johnson gives the students word problems, to which they must tell the answers in a sentence. The students also perform "board races": students work at their seat on a problem. After a squeak and a clack of slate pencils, they hold their slates up as soon as they finish. Then Mrs. Johnson poses some riddles, and students remember to stand when they address their teacher and guess the answer. Mrs. Johnson mentions the "elocution, speeches, and poems contest" to be held at the box social. Finally, Mrs. Johnson has students say a few "tongue twisters."

RECREATION AND LUNCH

In an age prior to electronics, students and teachers would know lots of ways to amuse themselves during wet weather. Mrs. Johnson has access to this folklore form known as oral history interviews. Passed from person to person, people share folk games that have not been formally taught as part of a curriculum. Students try an indoor game that includes the jingle:

> Tapping on the ice box
> Tapping on the spot
> I'll draw the circle
> And I'll punch the dot

The students must first establish what an icebox is and how it works, then they determine what the jingle is telling them to do. The game is similar to "Duck, Duck, Goose."

Students learn how to fold paper to form paper cups so they can get drinks of water from the water bucket. They learn about the outhouse, although the modern school lavatories are available. Mrs. Johnson moves a bench outside so the students can wash their hands with lye soap before lunch; she tells them how to make lye soap as they wash with it. Students eat lunches they brought from home, which in 1900 were packed in baskets, tin pails, or simply wrapped in newspaper or wax paper. Students placed some items in small glass jars. Students brought food such as meat, cheese, or peanut butter sandwiches on homemade bread, cookies, pie, cake, fruit, carrots, fried chicken, biscuits, meat, cornbread, or other homemade items. The drink for the day is water pumped from the well, dipped from the drinking bucket, and served in tin cups from the schoolhouse.

After lunch, it is time for games of marbles, tug of war, jacks, and stickball. Other individual games include hoops, cup and ball, and whimediddle (Kalman, 1982). A whimediddle is a wooden folk toy consisting of a dowel rod with notches cut into the top with a flat piece of wood attached to the end with a small tack that rotates freely like a propeller. A skilled person rubs a second small dowel rod across the notches to make the propeller change directions on command. Mrs. Johnson rings the bell signaling that students should pick up their belongings and clean out their desks. She asks the students to fold their hands and close their eyes as she counts backward from three to zero. In the stillness there is only the ticking of a mechanical clock, and then they are back in modern times—a group of third-grade students ready to go home after a very special day of school.

ASSESSMENT

When the students return to their modern classroom, they start a two-day writing assignment about what they learned during their time travel. They compare their life at Hope School with their day at Simmons School, pointing out similarities and differences. "I learned that there were double desks there! I also learned they ate lunches that they had to bring from home. I also learned that at that time the president was President McKinley. I learned about the old days." Often, students appear to have strengthened their sense of community by engaging in this simulation. They have been given an opportunity to use drama, games, and old-fashioned slate work to experience events from their community's past. These students have learned about history by living it. Together with their classmates and their teacher, they have traveled back in time.

CONCLUSIONS

Students need to find out about their community through experiences that allow them to relive events. Students develop their class community by engaging in common events and sharing experiences that allow them to explore the past. Students use dramatic experiences and events from their community's past. These students learn history that applies to their lives, and they learn about the people, sometimes even their relatives, who live in their town. Students learn about history by experiencing a small segment of it in great detail through drama.

Teachers want to expose students to history at an early age so that students have an adequate context for understanding. Teachers use drama to encourage historical thinking and deep learning about topics under study in the social studies class. Teachers want students to connect with their community, to understand what happened in it, and appreciate how it operated a century ago. Teachers give the students opportunities to explore a bit of educational history and philosophy when students get to compare their education to schools of the past. Teachers enjoy watching students' reaction to living a day in the past.

Community members also find this type of education to be valuable for their students because the students discover how they connect to the town. The community members have their history taught to the students, and the students form another type of community that learns together about their town. This community enjoys learning how they connect. The history of the community, taught through drama, compares educational systems to help students learn about school one hundred years ago and compare it with that of today.

THOUGHT QUESTIONS

1. What questions could students ask their parents and grandparents after this experience?
2. How could the teacher follow this experience by using oral history?
3. How could the students take what they have learned into the community?

NOTES

1. Reprinted with permission from the National Council for the Social Studies. Morris, R. V. (2002). Third grade at Simmons Elementary School, ca.1900. *Social Studies and the Young Learner, 14*(4), 6–10.

2. The One Room School House Committee, comprising members of the community, raised $40,000 to refurbish the building and move it onto

school grounds in 1989. Class rentals began in 1992. The building is self-sustaining, based on a fee of $25 per visit charged to teachers from outside Hope school who use it. It is free to the local classes. The committee also collected donations, hosted a bake sale, sold inscribed bricks, and received a small grant (under $5,000) from charitable groups, including the Indiana Historic Landmarks Foundation and the Bartholomew County Heritage Fund. The Indiana Gas Company provided heating and air conditioning systems. Many people also provided in-kind labor contributions, bringing the total cost of the project to about $120,000.

3. A teacher can portray the "schoolmarm" herself using resource materials and training provided by the One Room School House Committee, or she may hire a schoolmarm for the day. Teacher resources include Dixon, H. M. (1987). *Hope & Hawcreek Township: Its history and people.* Bartholomew County, IN; Taft-Carr, C., Johnson, B., Newman, B., Voorhies, L., & Webster, L. (1999). *Simmons School teacher's manual and resource guide.* Hope, IN: Flat Rock-Hawcreek School Corporation.

References

Catterall, J. S. (2007). Enhancing peer conflict resolution skills through drama: An experimental study. *Research in Drama Education, 12*(2), 163–178.

Clark, A. D. (2000). Living the past at Oak Hill School. *Now and Then, 17*(3), 13–17.

Clegg, Jr., A. A. (1991). Games and simulations in social studies education. In J. P. Shaver (Ed.), *Handbook of research on social studies teaching and learning* (pp. 523–529). New York: Macmillan.

Collins, C. S., & Eriksson, C. W. (1996). *The world of the little house.* New York: Scholastic.

Downey, M. T., & Levstik, L. S. (1991). Teaching and learning history. In J. P. Shaver (Ed.), *Handbook of research on social studies teaching and learning* (pp. 400–410). New York: Macmillan.

Edinger, M. (2005). The Pilgrim maid and the Indian chief. *Educational Leadership, 63*(2), 78–81.

Fines, J., & Verrier, R. (1974). *The drama of history: An experiment in cooperative teaching.* London: New University Education.

Goalen, P., & Hendy, L. (1993). 'It's not just fun, It works!' Developing children's historical thinking through drama. *Curriculum Journal, 4*(3), 363–384.

Hahn, C. L. (1998). *Becoming political: Comparative perspectives on citizenship education.* Albany, NY: State University of New York Press.

Kalman, B. (1982). *Early schools.* New York: Crabtree.

Kelin, D. A. (2002). To feel the fear of it: Engaging young people in social education. *Talking Points, 14*(1), 10–14.

McGuffey's Eclectic Spelling Book. (1879). New York: Van Nostrand Reinhold.

Morris, R. V., & Welch, M. (2000). *How to perform acting out history in the classroom.* Dubuque, IA: Kendall/Hunt.

National Council for the Social Studies. (1994). *Expectations of excellence: Curriculum standards for social studies.* Washington, D.C.: Author.

The New England Primer. (1805). Albany, NY: Whiting, Backus, & Whiting. http://www.sacred-texts.com/chr/nep/

Tanner, C. K. (2001). Into the woods, wetlands, and prairies. *Educational Leadership, 58*(7), 64–66.

Wilson, H. C. (2000). Discovery education: A definition. *Horizons, 19,* 25–29.

Chapter Four

———————O———————

Fourth Grade Civil War[1]

THE SOLDIERS IN THE CIVIL WAR fought for the liberation of a group of people whom they did not know well—they fought a war for justice. After the Emancipation Proclamation, the common people, these same soldiers who had fought in the Civil War, held uncommon ideals for the purpose of the war. The lives of most students are pretty common; they can connect, however, with a group of people, many of whom were their age and held high ideals. Students question some of their ideas when they explore the Civil War. Students think about their future and the world where they live (Tallent-Runnels & Yarbrough, 1992). Unfortunately, George and Scheft (1998) find that students are negative toward the future, and their pessimism has increased over the past twenty years. At a time when children see their world though pessimistic lenses, it is important for them to realize that others who shared common lives or common situations have risen to do uncommon deeds and share uncommon ideals. The imperiled nation survived because of a commitment to great ideals such as democratic processes and the abilities of people to see self-interest in community action as the common good. In this article students examine a group of common people, a social history, to find what made them uncommon. Moreover, students realize that big ideas many times intertwine with the thoughts and actions of a generation.

To communicate these ideas and to do a successful first-person historic presentation requires a teacher who is willing to take risks in front of the members of the class. In preparation for a Civil War presentation, the teacher dresses as a Civil War soldier while the students act as recruits who muster into the Union Army. The teacher tells the character's story in the first person by using the pronouns *I*, *my*, *me*, and *we*. Through first-person historical presentations, teachers can communicate ideas, conflicts, perceptions, and biases from the time. The teacher uses first-person presentation with other methods to help students learn.

When students recently recreated a Civil War muster, they explored content from the early days of the Civil War after the attack on Fort Sumter. The class established the state fair grounds setting at Camp Morton. Students experienced recruiting speeches and filled out their muster papers before gathering their gear and boarding the train south in anticipation of their approaching year in the army. For the Civil War soldier early in the war, this was the common method of induction. The teachers used this process to signal the beginning of the students' journey into the Civil War.

RATIONALE

To communicate, to interpret, to recreate, and show perspective—these are all goals of public historians. First-person historical presentations share these strengths. Public historians have used first-person characterizations in their interpretations of historic sites or explored history through reenactment for many years (Anderson, 1984, 1985, 1991; De Jonge, 1994; Jackson, 2000; Roth, 1998; West, 2001). Through using first-person presentation, interpreters can have a historic person interact with their audience. Present-day visitors can question the historical figures. Johnson (1995) created resources to help teachers and others develop historical characters. People need resources to improve their first-person skills. Interpreters can use skills to enliven historical, sociological, and psychological content. Teachers use first-person historical presentations as a way to help their students learn social studies standards. Many links between first-person presentations connect "Time, Continuity, and Change"; "Individuals, Groups, and Institutions"; and "Individual Identity and Development" (NCSS, 1994). Teachers use first-person historical presentations as a way to help their students learn social studies standards. Teachers use first-person skills in a variety of ways. They might experiment with first-person historical presentations as an extension of theater education (Catterall, 2007; Wagner, 1976) and as an interesting way to learn social studies (Fines & Verrier, 1974; Suiter & Meszaros, 2005). Teachers use it to generate interest or to hook their students on a topic. While several teachers use this method, they do so in isolation. They have neither network nor peers to share information with. Although Chilcoat (1996) and Morris and Welch (2000) find that many people report using drama in the social studies classroom through anecdotes, and recent publications have come forth (Fennessey, 2000; Taylor, 1998), very little research existed. Teachers use first-person presentations to communicate and interpret ideas to students. Teachers use first-person presentations to recreate time, place, and events. They use first-person presentations to demonstrate different perspectives that may be so foreign to their students that they may be disconcerting.

Teachers also help students to create their own first-person presentations. Students at various levels have different competencies when creating first-person characters. Colby's (1988; Cruz & Murthy, 2006) research describes how adolescents created their own first-person historical presentations. Students in the middle grades have many abilities to perform first-person historical presentations and demonstrate few inhibitions compared to other ages. Of course, primary grades can very easily do this as well. Teachers of the primary grades are familiar with story telling and have experience using role-playing with their students.

Teachers use first-person presentations to help students access information from multiple sources. Students hear information, see detail in clothing and artifacts, and read primary sources. In learning about the Civil War, students see how soldiers in the Civil War joined the army, discover what army life was like, and learn why men as well as boys decided to join the army. A first-person presentation helps students ask and answer these questions in the context of the life of an individual. A student remembers what soldiers said in a discussion or story, how they acted, and how they demonstrated the operation of the equipment. At the end of such a lesson it is reasonable to expect students to list why the soldiers enlisted and evaluate the most important reasons that motivated them to join. They would describe how a soldier enlisted and evaluate whether the young soldier's parent would let him go. They list the items that a soldier carried and evaluate if they could physically carry the amount required. Students describe camp life in the Civil War, analyze how soldiers would spend their time, and then work with complexity when they take the perspective of a soldier in the war. How has the war changed them so that they now are ready to accept a war as a war to end slavery—a war to make all men equal in the eyes of the law? Students compare the perspective and experience of the common soldier to the civilian. What experiences have the civilians had that make them ready to accept this new focus of the war? Finally, students take the perspective of a movie director. Is there any way to get a movie audience to see and feel the changes that have affected a soldier after two or four years of war?

DAY ONE AND BEYOND

Corbin (1988) describes her experiences in conducting first-person presentations and gives advice on how to construct a presentation. Corbin suggests the actor remain in character until the very end of the presentation. Drake and Corbin (1993) describe how they infuse questions into their presentations by seeding the audience. The seed questions act as a model of the type of appropriate questions to ask, and they break the ice in a large silent group. This seeding of questions generates additional questions from the audience. The planting of seeds in the context of a press conference helps people to take a role in the audience. Students write out the questions they wish to ask; the teacher helps the students write divergent questions to encourage the soldier to talk. The students take notes on the responses to their questions and to the questions that their friends ask. The questions they generate are the richest part of the first-person program, because the written student questions stimulate additional questions.

The first thing the teacher must do is to establish the setting to help the students know where they are in time and space. The students want to know: how did the audience, the recruits, and the recruiter in first person get here? To produce a meaningful setting the teacher must describe and make connections through vivid descriptions illustrating similarities and dissimilarities between that time period and the present. For example, the teacher can describe the present state fair grounds or state capitol, including details no longer present and calling attention to differences from a century ago. The teacher must work hard to include things and events that make the setting meaningful to the students; once students have this information they will be ready to accept the first-person characterization. Then the teacher will give a short background lecture about the character whom the student is portraying, including why the character is fighting in the war. Reference to the big issues of the day help prepare the students so they can understand what feelings and attitudes the people in the nation are thinking and arguing about. Students must search in depth to confront an unanswered question: why did the North and the South seemingly bumble into war over the question of slavery? The South says it will secede if the North elects a president who vows to halt slavery from entering the territories. The North has heard the South threaten to secede before, and every time the South backs down. Were there no attempts at compromise?

Next, the teacher starts the muster roll, and the students want to know how and where their commanding officer recruited them. For the muster roll, the students need to stand in line to receive a photocopy of an actual muster form, which they complete. The character asks the student/soldiers if they can read or write. Since nine out of ten soldiers in the Northern army could read, only a few recruits needed to just make their mark. How will they find out what this document says if they cannot read or speak English? What do they promise to do? Why is this important information? Students realized that not knowing the language or being unable to read could lead to some very frightening and uncomfortable situations.

Students come next to the section about underage enlistment in the primary source; soldiers had to be at least eighteen years old to serve in the armed forces. Students talk about whether their parents would let them go off to war as a minor, and they can generate arguments to persuade their parents to let an older brother go to war or to stay home. How can you get into the army if you are underage? Are there other ways to get into the army if you are underage? A father would need to sign for a minor to go to war, or the minor could bend the truth. Young people wrote "18" on a piece of paper and placed it in the heel of their shoe so they could say they were "over 18" (Wiley, 1952). The teacher asks the students if they think this is lying about their age, and students speculate about why someone would go to these lengths to enter the army. What should the army do with a minor caught lying to become a soldier? Should there be any different punishment for a boy who is only sixteen years old saying he is eighteen compared to one who is only one month shy from being eighteen? Students need to consider what is ethical in these situations when they make decisions.

Next the medical inspection occurs; surgeons provided medical care handicapped by the knowledge of the time period and hindered by patriotism. Many times medical officers conducted these inspections in mass, at night, or with less than rigorous interest. The inspector might turn his back, inspect at night, or inspect the entire group from a distance in order to utter the words, "I don't see any reason why these men could not serve in the Union Army" (Catton, 1951, 1952, 1953). Ask the students what immediate- and long-term problems this type of inspection would cause and why medical officers did inspections like this. Students generate answers about health care, spread of disease, and excitement or eagerness for a cause. They comment on how the ethics and the integrity of the community suffered, causing all the members to suffer. While it might seem like a minor problem, it had major implications. When the ranks thinned by the weak falling away from infirmities caused by the rigors of camp life, the army was left with regiments that were understrength. The teacher observes the students' decisions in these issues and their intricate rationales for their decisions. First-person presentation is an opportune time to pose ethical dilemmas with which students must wrestle. Issues of conscious truth, national emergency, community expectation, and individual right all play a role in these discussions.

The teacher briefly reviews what equipment the character carries and who provides it, and then the teacher asks the students what personal items they would carry. Included in this information is what the soldier eats and how he receives payment. Students make meaningful connections with Civil War soldiers when they see similar and dissimilar things that they would have eaten. When a teacher confronts students with information that is asynchronous with the details of their life or how they understand events or relationships, the students must struggle with the information to modify, accommodate, or reject these understandings. Because many students are familiar with what it takes to go camping or spend the night at a friend's house, they can make the connections that they would be required to carry everything they need with them on a march or in the field.

By asking, "How will you get to the front?" students respond to the opportunity to talk about marching and trains in the Civil War. Ask students why people had to march and why everyone could not walk at their own pace. After allowing the students to briefly experiment with marching in formation, they will experience how much they depend on the members of their group to be successful. The typical day included time for drill in marching and battlefield formations that facilitated rapid deployment or protection against different types of attack. The Civil War was a modern war in many ways, and technology in transportation was a major factor. Students can draw graphs showing railroad mileage in bar graph forms or showing railroad construction by decade. Students can also draw maps showing troop movements of Sherman's men or Stonewall's Foot Cavalry, emphasizing that these groups walked to cover this territory. This generation was the most traveled of any group of citizens in America up to that time; they had walked to explore much of the United States. If students get the opportunity to take a hike, they can compare this mileage with what an infantry unit would do in one day or one week.

Many of the men who enlisted in the 19th Indiana Infantry came from the area where the fourth-grade students live and attend school. A significant number of primary sources document this group of soldiers, and they reveal interesting stories about their lives during the Civil War. Private John Lindley, a composite character, represents the men of that outfit. Illustrated through multiple primary sources, a composite character is based upon several different soldiers rather than one individual. The presenter can then tell their story without being constrained by missing primary sources.

When President Lincoln called for volunteers, Governor Oliver P. Morton organized the group called the Black Hat Brigade for their distinctive headgear. They later earned the nickname of the Iron Brigade. Everyone was joining the Union army; they wanted to put down rebellion and see the world. The issue of slavery, however, was not foremost in their minds (McPherson, 1988). They organized with men from Wisconsin and Michigan and went east as the only all-western brigade in the Army of the Potomac. This is a group with many stories that can easily capture the imagination of the students; while at the same time it connects national events with local people and places.

While the purpose of the presentation is neither entertainment nor humor, the interjection of some humorous anecdotes holds the attention of the audience. Anecdotes can help point out conflicting values as a variety of men formed a community under the imposition of army regulation. Of all the formal army training and all the old army equipment the men hated was wearing their gaiters, or spats, the most. One morning Col. Gibbon came out to see his horse wearing gaiters, too (Nolan, 1983). This story illustrates the tension produced between the established army and its officers and how discipline was handled, with the sudden influx of young, rural volunteers. Students get the opportunity to identify individual, groups, or institutions in conflict with one another in these short but true tales.

In another incident, the men of the Black Hat Brigade saw the elephant, or battle, at the Battle of Brawner's Farm before Second Manassass. Here they stood in the open and fired at point blank range at their opponents; at the end of the battle, their dead had fallen with their heels lined up in a row tracing their rank of fire. Students question their bravery, and the bravery required of these men from both sides to stand exposed firing at one another. The Midwest soldiers went on to fight at the battle of South Mountain where they won the title the Iron Brigade, and they fought on the first day of Gettysburg (Foote, 1986a; 1986b; 1986c). They took such high casualties that they never possessed the power of a group again; their brigade literally was shot apart. Students have definite ideas after this experience, and they will want to share them.

Students many times forget the role of conscientious objectors in times of conflict. Students can write responses to such questions as this: if you were a member of the Brethren, Mennonite, or Quaker faiths, how would you respond to this situation? These groups have a long tradition of resisting war and violence. Students consider if it was easy for an individual to go west and thereby evade military service. Students question the role that conscientious objectors play in society viewed as heroes or cowards. Conscientious objectors can act as the conscience of a society when individuals call the views of a warring or violent people into question.

Another question that offers students an opportunity to challenge some of their assumptions and requires that they defend their point of view has to do with literacy. For example, if one army had a literacy rate of one in ten and the other had a literacy rate of one in three, would this make any difference in the results of the war? These students examine different army jobs: infantry, quartermaster signal corps, or medical corps. They make a decision whether they think literacy is important in each job. Then they consider the officers for each group and whether the officers needed to be literate. At the end of the war, General Robert E. Lee had lost a lot of his junior officers. The students must consider how these junior officers could have been replaced.

The teacher concludes the muster roll when the students fold and tie the muster papers with red ribbon or red tape before sending them to the state capitol. These small packets of paper fit easily into the cubbyholes of the desk and paper files of that time. This red ribbon gives us the phrase for government work "all tied up in red tape." State archives hold many records from the Civil War, and these records are a great resource for students researching the Civil War veterans from their community. Depending on the state, the students may be the first people to open the records since the Civil War. If this is true, that fact will hook the students into wanting to know more about the topic. These papers still wrapped in the faded red ribbon of a century ago lie waiting in state capitols or state libraries for students to discover.

Day Two

On another day the students can compare the Union army with that of the South, through a first-person presentation of a soldier from the Stonewall Brigade. The Stonewall Brigade was a crack outfit as was the Iron Brigade, and these soldiers fought against each other at Brawner's Farm and at South Mountain. It makes sense that they would speak as opponents to give opposing views of the same events. One soldier from the Confederate army and one from the Union Army can tell what motivated them to join their particular army. He can then compare how his experience in the army of his choice is similar to or differs from that of his opponent's army. Students can question both soldiers to compare answers about life on the home front, politics, or national growth and development in spite of the war.

Day Three

At this point the teacher explains a typical day in the Union army, the amount of free time, and what soldiers did for amusement. After providing the students with the lyrics to some of the Civil War songs, such as "The Battle Cry of Freedom," "John Brown's Body," or "All Quiet Along the Potomac" (Wiley, 1943), the students catch on quickly and join in singing. There are also a number of good recordings that provide instrumental music from this period. The lyrics, tempos, rhythm, instrumentation, and melody tell us much about the people who composed, performed, and listened to these works. Ask the students to predict what made these songs popular and what these songs told about the soldiers. Ask the students which songs remain popular and why they think the songs remain popular.

Day Four

The teacher also can use video clips to illustrate ideas that are not shown in a first-person presentation. Teachers can present ideas such as camp life, the marching army, naval engagements, balloons, fortifications, and medical care by just showing a videotape of these events. Video clips from films such as *Blue and Gray*, *Gettysburg*, *Glory*, *Gone with the Wind*, *A Stillness at Appomattox*, and Ken Burns's *Civil War* illustrate specific points. At their best, reenactors and movie producers can create an illusion of the Civil War on a scale that small groups of reenactors could not hope to replicate. Students can see items not regularly reenacted, restored, or replicated at historic sites. The video component fleshes out a student's experience with an additional way to get information not provided through first-person experiences.

Day Five

After the first four days, the students had an opportunity to see the battle flags of the brigade as well as other flags located downtown in the war memorial. On the steps of the state capitol, the returning troops gave these flags to the state for perpetual care. Many states have their Civil War battle flags restored and on display. This reverence for what is real transfers into the students' desire to discover an absolutely truthful version of history. Multiple artifacts representing multiple people and their perspectives need to be available to help students see that a first-person presentation only shows one side of a story.

Day Six

Finally students can complete individual research on Civil War or related topics. Those who want to find out more about the Civil War can look at the following topics: while the Civil War occurred, what other things happened in America? Social justice was a concern of a few social reformers at that time, but the conscription law was so flagrantly biased as to set off draft riots. Evaluate the phrase, "Rich man's war—poor man's fight." How did it originate? Is it justified? What events triggered riots at other times? Students look for depth of information when they search for patterns. The students make connections between riots in the North and the South at this time and then connect those riots to riots at other places at other times. Students who take on this topic find information illustrating social issues in the United States.

At this time another issue intertwined with the first—the expansive growth of the nation during the war. The nation grew and developed so much during this time that after four years, people could almost forget that they were in the same country. Students look at the complexity of interdisciplinary concepts and the nature of life in America in the 1860s to explore business, higher education, the Homestead Act, immigrants, industry, Native American policies, railroads, and western migration. While it is important for students to know about political and military history, it is equally important to consider the other issues that focused on expansive growth. These growth issues propelled America into the last half of the century.

Students looking at equity or representation issues compare who made up the army of the 1860s with the army of the twenty-first century. How has the army changed from the past to the present? When students examine this question, they look at public policy across a hundred-plus-year span to find out how national perceptions have changed to allow more groups access to the military and what groups the military establishment has yet to welcome. Students examine complexity of events across time when they examine the all-volunteer armies of 1860 and the twenty-first century. Who joined then and now and what is the motivation for enlistment? During the Civil War Lincoln eventually allowed black troops to fight but not in integrated units. Women did fight during the Civil War but not openly.

Day Seven

Students use notes in producing after-the-event journal reflections about the experience, or students create letters from the soldiers describing life in the Union army. Students can include information describing how and why a soldier enlisted, items that a soldier carried, and what camp life was like in the Civil War. In their letters students talk about how their ideas have changed in the time they have been in the army. They may explain that they started wanting to preserve the Union and became convinced they need to free the slaves. They may also wish to talk about originally wanting to reunite the Union but having become convinced that the South should be punished along the lines the Radical Republicans suggested.

Conclusions

Teachers can use a first-person characterization to communicate social history, which is the history of the common people. Students have obligations to sift and sort through this information to accommodate social history into the picture of major events occurring nationally and locally. The focus of the presentation is not on the generals or the political leaders but on the people who do their jobs and those the headlines usually miss. Teachers help students make connections between first-person presentations and other methods to create a rich tapestry of understanding about places and time. These people represent powerful stories and voices too often not heard in any other places.

Teacher educators can help their students see that issues from the Civil War are still with us (Catton, 1986). Preservice teachers can access these issues with primary sources or first-person presentations. Characters from that time period did not all agree on the issues; conflicting views filled the public press and the minds of people even then. Teachers need to help students see multiple perspectives by portraying characters representing the different geographic, ethnic, social, economic, and political groups. Students can still argue about issues from the 1860s because these issues have not gone away. Some of these issues still persist in society today. Students study public controversy through historic characters and find insights into democratic processes and understanding on public discussion and issues.

Teachers can introduce students to a person from a particular time period who could not normally come as a guest speaker. This method allows for flexibility in creating guests for students to interview. When students gather stories, they must compare narratives, and they look toward other sources to confirm or negate their understandings. When students interview guests, they determine the source of the information; they can gather the story for themselves. They can then compare this narrative with other narratives from other sources. Think of the excitement if students compared first-person Civil War stories to stories told by veterans from other wars. Teachers need to continually help students look for different perspectives and examine issues from that time and the implications of those issues for today.

THOUGHT QUESTIONS

1. How does teaching about war change when the nation is in conflict with other countries as opposed to when the nation is at peace?
2. What pressures for censorship or self-censorship might exist for teachers in times of conflict?
3. Has the role of conscientious objectors changed across time?
4. What do conscientious objectors tell us about minority voices in history?

NOTE

1. Morris, R. V. (2001). Using first-person presentation to encourage student interest in social history. *Gifted Child Today*, 24(1), 46–53. Reprinted with the permission of Prufrock Press Inc. (http://www.prufrock.com)

REFERENCES

Anderson, J. (1991). *A living history reader.* Nashville, TN: American Association of State and Local History.

———. (1985). *The living history sourcebook.* Nashville, TN: American Association of State and Local History.

———. (1984). *Time machines: The world of living history.* Nashville, TN: American Association of State and Local History.

Catterall, J. S. (2007). Enhancing peer conflict resolution skills through drama: An experimental study. *Research in Drama Education, 12*(2), 163–178.

Catton, B. (1986). *America goes to war: An introduction to the Civil War and its meaning to Americans today.* New York: MJF Books.

———. (1953). *The Army of the Potomac: A stillness at Appomattox.* Garden City, NY: Doubleday.

———. (1952). *The Army of the Potomac: Glory road.* Garden City, NY: Doubleday.

———. (1951). *The Army of the Potomac: Mr. Lincoln's army.* Garden City, NY: Doubleday.

Chilcoat, G. W. (1996). Drama in the social studies classroom: A review of the literature. *Journal of Social Studies Research, 20*(2), 3–17.

Colby, R. W. (1988). *On the nature of dramatic intelligence: A study of developmental difference in the process of characterization by adolescents.* Unpublished doctoral dissertation, Harvard University, Cambridge.

Corbin, D. (1988). Using drama in the classroom. *The Councilor, 48* (October), 43–48.

Cruz, B. C., & Murthy, S. A. (2006). Breathing life into history: Using role-playing to engage students. *Social Studies and the Young Learner, 19*(1), 4–8.

De Jonge, M. (1994). *Staging battle: A performance analysis of military reenactment.* Unpublished Master's Thesis, University of Guelph, Ontario, Canada.

Drake, F., & Corbin, D. (1993). Making history come alive: Dramatization in the classroom. *Teaching History: A Journal of Methods, 18*(2), 59–67.

Fennessey, S. M. (2000). *History in the spotlight: Creative drama and theatre practices for the social studies classroom.* Portsmouth, NH: Heinemann.

Fines, J., & Verrier, R. (1974). *The drama of history: An experiment in cooperative teaching.* London: New University Education.

Foote, S. (1986a). *The Civil War: A narrative: Fort Sumter to Perryville.* New York: Vintage Books.

———. (1986b). *The Civil War: A narrative: Fredericksburg to Meridian.* New York: Vintage Books.

———. (1986c). *The Civil War: A narrative: Red River to Appomattox.* New York: Vintage Books.

George, P. G., & Scheft, T. (1998). Children's thoughts about the future: Comparing gifted and nongifted students after 20 years. *Journal for the Education of the Gifted, 21*(2), 224–239.

Jackson, A. (2000). Inter-acting with the past—The use of participatory theatre at museums and heritage sites. *Research in Drama Education, 5*(2), 199–215.

Johnson, C. (1995). *Who was I?: Creating a living history persona.* Excelsior Springs, MO: Fine Arts Press.

McPherson, J. M. (1988). *The battle cry of freedom: The Civil War era.* New York: Oxford University.

Morris, R. V., & Welch, M. (2000). *How to perform acting out history in the classroom to enrich social studies education.* Dubuque, IA: Kendall/Hunt.

National Council for the Social Studies. (1994). *Expectations of excellence: Curriculum standards for social studies.* Washington, D.C.: Author.

Nolan, A. T. (1983). *The Iron Brigade.* Ann Arbor: Historical Society of Michigan.

Roth, S. F. (1998). *Past into present: Effective techniques for first-person historical interpretation.* Chapel Hill: University of North Carolina Press.

Suiter, M., & Meszaros, B. T. (2005). Teaching about saving and investing in the elementary and middle school grades. *Social Education, 69*(2), 92–95.

Tallent-Runnels, M. K., & Yarbrough, D. W. (1992). Effects of the future problem solving program on children's concerns about the future. *Gifted Child Quarterly, 36*(4), 190–194.

Taylor, P. M. (1998). *Redcoats and patriots: Reflective practice in drama and social studies.* Portsmouth, NH: Heinemann.

Wagner, B. J. (1976). *Dorothy Heathcote: Drama as a learning medium.* Washington, D.C.: National Education Association.

West, R. M. (2001). Personalized interpretation and experience enhancement. *Informal Learning, 46,* 16–18.

Wiley, B. I. (1952). *The life of Billy Yank.* Baton Rouge: Louisiana State University Press.

———. (1943). *The life of Johnny Reb.* Baton Rouge: Louisiana State University Press.

Chapter Five

How First-person Historical Narrative is Conducted by Fourth and Fifth Grade Teachers

Two case studies reveal how and why elementary school teachers use first-person historical presentations as an instructional method in elementary school classrooms. When they use first-person presentations, teachers immediately hook the attention of students through the use of period clothing; teachers then integrate their characters into the unit of instruction. Students quickly become involved in some aspect of the first-person historical presentation, and assessment of a first-person historical presentation occurs within the context of the unit. All four of these categories—attention, involvement, assessment, and context—support the individual teachers who exhibit creativity in teaching social studies in the classroom. The implications lead to the support, encouragement, and improvement of the quality of first-person historical presentations in preservice and teacher in-service.

Elementary school social studies teachers conduct first-person historical presentations in their classrooms by dressing in period clothing or using props to establish their character. When they do this while teaching social studies, classroom teachers explore social history, which emphasizes the life of the common people; in first-person historical presentations teachers take on a role as a figure from the past. Elementary school teachers conduct first-person historical portrayals as a novel way to teach social studies to their students. By looking at common people through studying social history, students find out about working people rather than the wealthy, powerful, or famous. By focusing on common people, students can learn about women, minorities, and people who have lost their voice in history.

RATIONALE

To examine first-person historical presentations requires looking at the work of authors in three fields: museum studies, drama, and education. Peter Labor (1998) describes the use of living history in historical reenactments and museums. The use of first-person characters for educational purposes, however, remains outside the focus of his work. Clearly though teachers could use his ideas, which are brought from the field of museum studies, to enrich the teaching of social studies. While no research exists in the field, a drama scholar wrote a thesis about an adult military reenactment group. Stacey Roth (1998; Winston, 1999) discusses reenactment as dramatic narrative. She writes specifically to help re-enactors develop a character for a first-person event; developing the person includes getting a job, securing period clothing, and collecting details of alter egos. This very detailed book elaborates on multiple considerations in the construction of a historic persona. While these resources never specifically designated helping elementary school teachers, they certainly can provide background material for putting together first-person presentations in the classroom. The role of the museum as an edifying institution makes transitions from cultural interpretation to classroom instructor possible.

Drama education also affects education in first-person historical presentation. In drama presentations aesthetic development is the goal, but the values, content, and skills of social studies make for good contexts to explore dramatically. Dorothy Heathcote (Jackson 2000, Wagner, 1976) used drama as the first-person historical method to help students experience theater in drama education programs. It is important to point out that students are not expected to create theater stage plays; through role-playing the students react to situations contrived by the first-person character. When teachers ask students to examine social studies themes or concepts, students use drama to examine history or contemporary events illustrating different times, places, or cultures. Fines and Verrier (1974, Fennessey 2000) came from the drama tradition to write qualitative research about how they used drama to teach social studies in an elementary classroom. The students met a variety of characters and created their own character to interact and interpret historical events; they also used first-person techniques. Phillip Taylor (1998) comes from a theater perspective and compares the past with the present culture. Fifth-grade students used drama to explore events in Boston leading up to the American Revolution. From theatrical elements, assistance for peer group members exists in helping the individual define their place within a historical group. Students of different ages have different competencies when creating first-person characters. Morris (2000) describes how adolescents created their own first-person historical presentations. Students in the elementary middle grades have many abilities that allow them to perform first-person historical presentations successfully, and yet they have few inhibitions compared to other ages. It would be interesting to see if students with continuing drama experiences from preschool to high school would still have these same self-critical traits. Elementary students can certainly take roles as first-person characters to interpret a figure from a specific period in time.

Education gives scant research evidence on the conduct of first-person historical presentations, and few pieces exist to guide educators in creating their own characters. The work that does exist comes from the perspectives of museum studies, re-enactors, or drama. Phillip J. C. Elliot Wright (2000) describes his experiences in conducting first-person presentations, and he gives advice on how to construct a presentation. Elliot Wright (2000) and McCord (1995) suggest remaining in character until the very end and using children's books with the character. Roth (1998) describes how she infuses questions into her presentations by seeding the audience. The seed questions act as a model of the type of appropriate questions to ask; they break the ice in a large silent group. This seeding of questions generates additional questions from the audience. The planting of seeds in the context of a press conference helps people in the audience to assume a role in the educational process. Although a few reports of first-person presentations describe successful programs, research is sparse. For example, Chilcoat (1996) and Morris (2000, 2001, 2002a, 2002b) found that while many people reported using drama in the social studies classroom through antidotes, little research existed. Currently no research exists to directly substantiate the practice of teachers using first-person historic presentation in the elementary school classroom. Researchers have not directly addressed the effectiveness of this practice in education, and little research exists about the method outside education. Such unanswered questions exist as: who uses the method? When is it used? What do teachers do? Where do teachers use the method in instruction? How do teachers prepare for the lesson? Why do teachers feel that this method is valuable? As teachers answer these questions, their experiences will make creating first-person historic presentations easier for teachers who are ready to experiment with the method.

TWO CASE STUDIES

The two case studies presented here represent a number of interviews with teachers. All the teachers had heterogeneously grouped students in their classrooms; the students represented the approximate ethnic make up of the student population of the state. Mrs. Roush and Mr. Fouts are experienced fifth- and fourth-grade teachers in the same school district but in different buildings. They used state standards to create lessons appropriate for their grade in U.S. and state studies, and they both used multiple methods of instruction to help students learn. Both teachers used content from the American Revolution in their first-person historical presentations and cover National Council for the Social Studies standards (1994) [see appendix II]. Mr. Fouts meets these standards:

I. Culture
II. Time, Continuity, and Change
VI. Power, Authority, and Governance

Mrs. Roush meets these standards:

II. Time, Continuity, and Change
V. Individual Groups and Institutions
X. Civic Ideals and Practices

Many people use first-person historical presentations in their classrooms, but the researcher only selected elementary school teachers who use this method regularly and attempted to determine their perspectives. The goal was to compare the views of teachers who use this method as part of a sequence of instruction in their classroom versus inviting a guest into the classroom to portray a historical character. This selection insured that the first-person historical presentation was integrated with instruction. It was thought that a guest would pop in and out of a classroom without continuity or assessment. Teachers, who used this method as a part of their instructional program, however, could talk most effectively about how it worked with their students.

EVIDENCE

The method of first-person historical presentation is the logical extension of individual creativity in teaching elementary social studies. Teachers capture the attention of their students through period clothing. The students respond to the period clothing because it is unexpected in the normal life of the elementary school classroom. Teachers first need to know their audience; then they need to be able to capitalize on the sense of adventure, which they can create when they present students with an experience of something unknown. Mrs. Roush prepares her class for the unexpected when she says, "I am not going to behave like myself." In the minds of elementary school students this raises the possibility of the unexpected even more; Mr. Fouts talks about an unexpected prop that he uses. "I had a small scalp . . . because that was . . . the focus of the presentation." Students want to know about Mrs. Roush in her

historic and mysterious life and background; elementary students
see the adventure and mystery in a first-person historical presentation. The students in class with Mrs. Roush see her as the character she is portraying. In Mr. Fouts's class the students become so
excited by wanting to discover more about the mysterious character
that "Often kids would direct the course of where we were going."
Students' questions drive the content of the program at some point
as teachers peak student curiosity. The students ask question after
question; the teacher uses mystery and historic clothing to produce
a creative environment for social studies instruction.

The teacher integrates instruction using the first-person historic presentation within the unit; many times introductory lessons
precede the characterization. All teachers interviewed had very
clear ideas about what they wanted the class to learn, and they
had planned in great detail to help students accomplish that learning. Then the first-person historical presentation builds upon that
learning to help the students learn even more about the people and
events of that time. Mrs. Roush says that she usually has several
background lessons to build general information about the period
before she brings out a character. "Mrs. Roush introduces that
particular conflict and some of the issues involved in the war of
independence." Mr. Fouts says that the unit opens in chronological
fashion discussing the causes of the American Revolution before
the students form connections to the character. Teachers alternate
between establishing the big themes, issues, and connections with
what these events meant to individuals. Mr. Fouts says, "I also
tried to tie in little human interest stories." The background lessons
allow the teacher to creatively build additional content on exist-
ing schema. Personal detail hooked students into the storytelling
aspects of the first-person historical presentation.

What the teachers perceive the students are doing during the
presentation interested the researcher; teachers say that students
contrast life from the present to the past. Mrs. Roush asks them,
"Don't you agree?" When she does this, she purposely puts her
students in a situation where they must disagree. Mrs. Roush gets
students to question what life is presently like by asking the students to agree that her life is like their life and pointing out obvious

discrepancies between the past and the present in her questions. The students must question the character's statement and compare it to their life and evaluate it as being accurate for their time, place, and situation. Mr. Fouts uses video clips to do this; the teachers value the generation of student questions in the presentations. Mrs. Roush says, "That is the richest part of the lesson when the children generate questions." Mr. Fouts also moves into questions and answers. Students in both classes respond by showering their teacher with creative questions. Students' interest drove the content and the order of the presentation with students hungry to find out more detail than the teachers expected.

Teachers use assessment as part of the first-person historical presentation. It is very common for the students to end with a writing assignment; Mrs. Roush follows a presentation immediately with a reflective writing assignment. After a presentation Mr. Fouts says, "I . . . want them to do a journal entry." Students also engage in social studies projects after the presentation; in Mrs. Roush's classroom, students must create an end of the unit project. In Mr. Fouts's classroom, the students read and compare excerpts from primary source materials. Each class must interpret the assignment after the creative experience with the first-person historic presentation.

CASE STUDIES

Example Case 1: Mrs. Roush

To prepare a lesson, Mrs. Roush reads biography and primary sources; she then chooses a specific moment from Abigail Adams's life to portray. Next, she tries a variety of ways to experiment with the character. She gets silly with it, tries the character on, attempts to get inside the character, picks up a pen and writes in Abigail's voice, and finally imagines Abigail Adams responding to a variety of situations. All this helps Mrs. Roush feel more in tune with the way the character thought and helps her determine the language that she will use in the presentation.

Generally I choose the period of about six weeks right after her husband left the office of the presidency. She returns to their home in Braintree six weeks before he left the White House, and I choose that time period when she's there preparing for his retirement from public office . . . I can talk about all the events that she was involved in during the events that [led] up to the writing of the Declaration of Independence, her stand on Women's Rights, and the time in France when her husband was serving in the delegation to France. (Mrs. Roush, individual interview)

Not only does Mrs. Roush have a variety of themes in public life with which she can work, but she can also focus on change in a private life. Only after she has read and experimented with all of these ideas is Mrs. Roush ready to present her character.

The lessons serve as introductory lessons, but she usually has several background lessons to build up general information about the period before she brings out a character. She uses these to define issues, establish location, and determine the period of time. Mrs. Roush feels that the students need to know ahead of time what the presentation is about because otherwise "it is just their silly teacher dressing up and doing something goofy." She makes sure they know ahead of time that they are going to do something that is a little bit different, something that is fun for the entire class, but they also realize that Mrs. Roush wants them to learn something. She needs to establish herself as a character different from a teacher. "When I come in I am not going to look like myself. I'm not going to behave like myself. You will need to relate to me as the person that I'm portraying." She tries to prepare the students for both the surprise of different clothing and the surprise of different ideas and attitudes when they speak to a new character. The students get accustomed to meeting new people with ideas that are foreign to theirs. Just as important the students in her class meet people who look peculiar, and they quickly adapt to these differences.

Mrs. Roush makes every minute count; she wants to make sure that the students focus on learning ideas rather than fixating on the clothing. She does not want them to see funny people performing in strange costumes. Two of her characters have fairly elaborate costumes, but the other two do not. They are fairly simple costumes, but they really help to get students into the spirit of the character and get the students to see her "as the character not as Mrs. Roush who is going to be grading their math paper in an hour." She uses the clothing as a symbol to help the students understand that she is speaking as someone with a different perspective. Once the student establishes that the teacher is a different character, the teacher can then help her students understand her unique ideas that may be different from their own.

Mrs. Roush portrays several characters: Priscilla Garth Chadwick portrays the events of 1760–1780 in Chadds Ford, Pennsylvania; Abigail Adams; and a local woman named Susanna Barns, who portrays the Underground Railroad activity of the 1830s. A couple of composite fictional characters complete the multiple personalities of Mrs. Roush.

> For the first ten to fifteen minutes I just talk to them about the character that I'm portraying: Who I am, the time period in which I live, my family, my background, and some of my beliefs. Then I start asking the children questions about their life and time period. Since all of the characters that I portray are women who had children, I make some statement about one of my children and ask them "Don't you agree? Don't you find that so for your life?" and deliberately set up a conflict situation so they have to say, "Well, no it's not like that at all." They get pulled into it and get involved [by] asking questions. That is the richest part of the lesson when the children generate questions. (Mrs. Roush, individual interview)

The students do respond to the character by picking up the social and personal clues she drops for them; this does not surprise the students. Very quickly the students suspend their disbelief and interact with her as another character. Besides thinking skills, Mrs. Roush builds connections to specific content into her lessons; Priscilla Garth Chadwick, who was from Chadds Ford, lived near the Battle of Brandywine. Some of the officers on General Washington's staff used her farmhouse during the Battle of Brandywine, so Mrs. Roush introduces that particular conflict and some of the issues involved in the war for independence.

Mrs. Roush follows a presentation immediately with a reflective writing assignment, or sometimes she asks the students to write a letter to the character. Mrs. Roush tries to help the students imagine in their mind that the character is real, and in doing this students sometimes generate additional questions for the character. If they have really engaged with the character, feel as if they knew the person, and want to continue a discussion, that dialogue becomes the subject of their writing. If the level of engagement is not quite so pronounced, then the students do a more personal reflection in the journal, perhaps as a compare and contrast essay. In this assignment students compare a couple of different characters through first-person presentations.

Students must create an end-of-unit project, and many students do first-person presentations. Usually after having shared the third major character about the women who worked locally with the Underground Railroad, Mrs. Roush asks the students to learn more about the local community at the same time or choose someone from elsewhere in the United States during this time. The students can develop a short presentation about that person, become involved in research, and go to the County Historical Association. The CHA has a good library that has some great artifacts, old newspapers, and journals about community members. The students get to access some of those materials.

For the presentation, which the students develop themselves, they decide with Mrs. Roush what the rubric for the assignment is going to be. The class creates a checklist together, "What are we going to look for in a really good presentation?" Then the students evaluate their peers. Most of the students

Table 5.1. First-person Rubric

Score Possible Points	Category Criteria
	Personal Detail
_____ (4)	Links to the common person, anecdotes that reflect on the character of the individual and that reflect on the character of their friends
_____ (3)	Anecdotes that reflect on the character of their friends and that reflect on the character of the individual
_____ (2)	Anecdotes that reflect on the character of the individual
_____ (1)	Generalities
	Content Accuracy
_____ (3)	Disclaimer of legends or myths, alternative interpretation, and accurate content
_____ (2)	Alternative interpretation and accurate content
_____ (1)	Accurate content
_____ (0)	Misinformation or misconceptions
	Context
_____ (3)	Establish time and place, connect the character to an idea that transcends the time, and connect the character to an idea that defines the time
_____ (2)	Establish time and place and connect the character to an idea that defines the time
_____ (1)	Establish time and place
_____ (0)	Missing context
	Total Points
_____ (10)	

really want to develop a dramatic presentation themselves, but there are a few who are just not comfortable with that. Mrs. Roush still wants them to do research and to learn about an actual person during this period, but they may create a mock newspaper from the period or create a journal for the person instead. The rest of the class starts developing sources, notes, research, scripts, period clothing, and a presentation; the students who opt to do this really seem to enjoy themselves.

Example Case 2: Mr. Fouts

Mr. Fouts also uses sources for his presentation, though he is trying to find the time in the future to visit a large state university library to see if he can use some of the things they have in their archives. Mr. Fouts did not have access to primary documents; the above-mentioned university is several hours away by car, so it would require a major effort on his part to visit it. "I have been told [the local library] also has some information that is pretty first hand." He got a variety of secondary sources and started to see what seemed to be consistent among them. He also looked at how writers of historical fiction put together their narratives to see where drama, action, and details converge. "I hear [Allan] Eckert has an excellent book; I have not read that yet. I am reading *Long Knife*. I read all the parts I needed for my presentation, and I am going back through and reading in more detail." He realized that there are many legends mixed into the events. He decided not to be George Rogers Clark because to talk about himself seemed awkward, and he felt that he would need information to which he did not have access. Mr. Fouts portrayed Major Joseph Bowman, a friend of George Rogers Clark, and as Clark's captain he told about his experience of capturing Kaskaskia and Cahokia.

Mr. Fouts borrowed the full buckskin outfit top and bottom with fringe and bone buttons from a middle-school teacher. He also borrowed the clothing that he might have worn in a more social setting when not in the wilderness. He had a typical hat of the time, a hatchet, a knife made out of bear claw, a haversack, and a powder horn.

> I had a small scalp that was quite interesting because that was kind of the focus of the presentation. George Rogers Clark just did not take off to kill Indians. They were protecting the settlers. It all had to do with these scalps, so the center-piece—the whole idea of the scalping going back and forth, was the hook to get the kids' attention. (Mr. Fouts, individual interview)

The moccasins were more typical of Plains Indians, but he solved this dilemma by hiding the beads by tucking them into the buckskin. The real Pennsylvania rifle had a broken stock. It was not safe to fire, but all the parts worked so he could show the students how it worked.

The unit progressed in chronological fashion by discussing the causes of the American Revolution, the anger over the Proclamation of 1763, settlers moving across the Appalachians, and British leadership in cultivating good relationships with the Native Americans. Mr. Fouts turned his attention to the start of the American Revolution, and the class attacked the America Revolution in the West. The students read from the textbook, and the next day they discussed the evidence: where the documents came from, the actual George Rogers Clark mission, what role Bowman played, and where the story had holes. The textbook presented information chronologically, but from there he diverged from the text. Students got an opportunity to both examine primary sources and to question a representative from the past.

The first time Mr. Fouts did the program, he found his "nerves affected it a little bit," and he "kept getting bogged down with details." Mr. Fouts used segments from an Eastern National Park Service Association video about George Rogers Clark, maps, and digital scans of still images. He turned off the VCR sound to point out key details as he talked, and he paused when he needed to concentrate on a particular aspect of the story. Mr. Fouts reinforced the points he wanted to

illustrate; the video provided the students with pictures of Mr.
Fouts's story. Students got multiple media exposure to the
topic through VCR tapes, maps, artwork, artifacts, and narrative. The multiple media reinforced his commentary rather
than the media telling the story for him; the advantage of this
situation allowed the students to interject questions, comments, and statements.

Mr. Fouts started with three or four maps to help students get the big picture of location as he told the story. He
referred to the map, told the story, and looked at the video. He
supplemented all of this with digital reproductions of historic
or contemporary art created to interpret these events in addition to modern photos of the actual sites today. To prepare he
scanned pictures out of books from different perspectives, and
he created pictures to really focus on the faces or pull back
getting multiple points of view. When Mr. Fouts engages the
students in reading the face of the character in the artwork, it
helps the student to evaluate the visual evidence to interpret
what the character is thinking and feeling in this situation.

> For instance when the settlers were moving out west . . .
> coming across on the water, flooding the wagons, and then
> there was another one where they use a flat boat. We could
> talk about that [and] how George Rogers Clark came down
> to Corn Island on the flatboat. They can see all that as we're
> talking and they're not saying, "What's a flatboat?" (Mr. Fouts,
> individual interview)

Mr. Fouts develops vocabulary and concepts when he gives
the students multiple visual experiences; students hear a
description or definition, and at the same time they see an
image.

Mr. Fouts adds stories about people to interest elementary students. "I also tried to tie in little human interest stories
about the drummer boy where he was carried on one of the
men's shoulders because he was so small." Mr. Fouts believes

that students like to find out about people like themselves. Different people scare them slightly, but even scarier are people like themselves who commit atrocities. Mr. Fouts gets personal responses from the students when they talk about this part of the story. He says that when talking about scalping, the students say, "Wow, if that was happening to my friends and family I think I would be upset, too." Mr. Fouts believes that students make the connection from the events discussed in that class to their own lives; they realize that on the frontier the lives of their friends and family would have been in jeopardy. The multiple media presentation allows students to make connections across time as well as to explore interesting characters. He starts with the multiple media interactive talk and then moves into questions and answers.

Those questions deal with what he is wearing and how he fits into the period. During the second and third times that he made the presentations the details remained important, but student questions covered many of those details. "I didn't need to explain my outfit as much. That was all done as we went along, and often kids would direct the course of where we were going." Student curiosity, which was demonstrated through their questions, guides the pace and structure of the program; student questioning makes the teaching very conversational. Mr. Fouts feels that the size of the group, his proximity to the students, the personal presence, and the visual contact all help to establish his character.

> I think the smaller the group the better because it is very personal. I know one girl got confuse[d] as to whether I was supportive of the British or Americans, and I just said, "What are you talking about young lady? I'm not gonna fight with them; are you kidding me? They're scalping women and children." She was sitting there, "Sorry, sir." So I mean you can really get their eye contact. I think with the big group it's harder to maintain that. This is why I would stay small. (Mr. Fouts, individual interview)

Mr. Fouts tries to remain consistent to his character in everything that he does during his presentation. He neither breaks
character in his one-and-a-half hour program nor does he
jump back and forth between periods of history. He remains
a figure from his period in time.

The Indiana Historical Bureau puts out some pamphlets
detailing different aspects of George Rogers Clark; Mr.
Fouts uses one of these as a follow up to his presentation.
The pamphlet shows three different diary entries from Hamilton, Bowman, and Clark. The students read the excerpts
and can see that a scalping incident occurred outside the
fort just before Hamilton surrendered. It was interesting
for the students to talk about the incident from the British perspective. "These people were brutally murdered. It
was horrible. How could this happen?" From Clark and
Bowman's perspective the students talked about, "How we
tried to hold the men back but they were so angry because
of the loved ones that had been killed. The numbers killed
were completely different." The class compared the historical situation to different conflicting perspectives found today
where finding the truth is in doubt due to war, genocide, or
terrorism. Mr. Fouts evaluated his first-person presentation;
he thought and worked to improve it. The students looked
for consistencies like murdered Indians in front of the fort;
students found where documents agreed and disagreed; then
they had to draw their own conclusions. "Next year I probably would want to do a journal entry about 'What did you
find fascinating about Mr. Bowman's presentation? If you
had any other questions, what might they be?'" Mr. Fouts
wants students to also think about the presentation through
written responses to the character. Students could continue
to ask more reflective questions after asking more impul-
sive questions. Mr. Fouts exhibits a strong commitment to
historical methods and challenges students to use historical
evidence when the students compare primary sources.

The third time Mr. Fouts did the presentation at the
school he taped himself; he wanted to see how he could

improve. He used the VCR to see how he told his story and what parts attracted the most student interest.

> I think looking at my first time I did it and then the third time I was unhappy. I think I thought if I could have had a better grasp on the material the first time . . . it was not as good as I'd like for it to have been. This year I think it will just natural[ly] flow because I will know that character so well. [Last year] I felt held down by details because I was still learning them myself. (Mr. Fouts, individual interview)

Mr. Fouts has both experience and confidence with the story now that will allow him to relax when he tells it. He felt held back by content, and this year he anticipates struggling less with retention of the material. In communicating the events to students, he made the events his own; the students accepted the presentation as his story. "What I found was the more of a story I could tell the better it was." The multiple media story, which was both convincing and imaginative, helped him connect with his students, and his success has him looking forward to future characters. Mr. Fouts saw this as a successful program, and he saw his students being successful with it.

CONCLUSIONS

Fifth- and fourth-grade students who experienced social studies through first-person historical narrative seemed to grow in their understanding of content knowledge, and the students seemed to enjoy learning with the method, too. The multiple sensory stimulation of talking, listening, seeing, touching, and smelling helped them to develop strong questions. The students could use these experiences to increase their empathetic understanding about the people discussed in social studies class. Teachers do not know what their peers do with first-person presentation; however, they wonder what their peers think and perceive about their students and themselves as a result of using this method as a way of teaching social studies. There are few peers to talk with about doing first-person historical presentations.

While obviously these two case studies do not speak for all elementary- or middle-school social studies teachers, two implications do become evident from these case studies of classroom teachers for teachers interested in experimenting with this method. Classroom teachers remain isolated from one another, and there is little opportunity for sharing successes, creativity, strategies, and ways to improve. Teachers feel that they create curriculum and method by themselves. Once teachers feel that they have found methods, which they consider successful with their students, there are few ways to communicate their successes to their peers. Teachers in master's classes and in-service opportunities need to create forums for discussing how and when they use this method of teaching.

The implications for teacher-educators become clear. Instructors of methods classes need to provide preservice teachers with models of first-person historical presentations. Preservice teachers need experience giving first-person historical presentations in class, and then they need to give presentations with multiple ages of elementary students in field experiences. The preservice teacher needs to feel comfortable with the method before they have a classroom of their own. Some teachers in the field, who have experimented with the method, find first-person historical presentation important in helping them to teach their students.

Using the method of first-person historical presentation is the logical extension of individual creativity in teaching elementary social studies. Teachers immediately hook the attention of their students through period clothing, then teachers integrate the character into the instruction of the unit, and the students become involved in some aspect of the first-person historical presentation; and assessment occurs within the context of the unit. Teachers use the method of first-person historical presentations to offer students in elementary school classrooms an opportunity to enter into social studies experiences. While some readers might attribute the success of this method to novelty, these teachers know the benefits of utilizing a variety of teaching methods in the classroom. These teachers open the door to social history and beckon students to enter into the past with creative teaching practices.

THOUGHT QUESTIONS

1. What do you think about the scalping and reference to weapon models?
2. Do you want your students to disagree with you?
3. Who do you know that you could portray as a character?

REFERENCES

Chilcoat, G. W. (1996). Drama in the social studies classroom: A review of the literature. *Journal of Social Studies Research, 20*(2), 3–17.

Eckert, A. W. (2001). *The frontiersmen: A narrative*. Ashland, KY: Jesse Stuart Foundation.

Elliot Wright, P. J. C. (2000). *Living history*. London: Brassey's Inc.

Fennessey, S. M. (2000). *History in the spotlight: Creative drama and theatre practices for the social studies classroom*. Westport, CT: Heinemann.

Fines, J., & Verrier, R. (1974). *The drama of history: An experiment in co-operative teaching*. London: New University Education.

Jackson, A. (2000). Inter-acting with the past: The use of participatory theater at museums and heritage sites. *Research in Drama Education, 5*(2), 199–215.

Johnson, C. (1995). *Who was I?: Creating a living history persona*. Excelsior Springs, MO: Fine Arts Press.

Labor, P. (1998). The living heritage museum as an educational tool. *Pathways: The Ontario Journal of Outdoor Education, 10*(3), 10–12.

McCord, S. (1995). *The storybook journey: Pathways to literacy through story and play*. Old Tabor, NJ: Simon and Schuster.

Morris, R. V. (2002a). Presidents' Day in second grade with first-person presentation. *Gifted Child Today, 25*(4), 26–29, 64.

———. (2002b). Third grade at Simmons Elementary School, ca. 1900. *Social Studies and the Young Learner, 14*(4), 6–10.

———. (2001). Using first-person presentation to encourage student interest in social history. *Gifted Child Today, 24*(1), 46–53.

———. (2000). The history walk: Integrated multi-age learning. *Gifted Child Today, 23*(4), 22–27, 53.

National Council for the Social Studies. (1994). *Expectations of excellence: Curriculum standards for social studies.* Washington, D.C.: Author.

Roth, S. F. (1998). *Past into present: Effective techniques for first-person historical interpretation.* Chapel Hill: University of North Carolina Press.

Taylor, P. (1998). *Redcoats and patriots: Reflective practice in drama and social studies.* Portsmouth, NH: Heinemann.

Thom, J. A. (1994). *Long knife.* New York: Ballantine Books.

Wagner, B. J. (1976). *Dorothy Heathcote: Drama as a learning medium.* Washington, D.C.: National Education Association.

Winston, J. (1999). Theorizing drama as moral education. *Journal of Moral Education, 28*(4), 459–471.

Chapter Six

———————O———————

Sixth Grade at Hope, Indiana, Cemetery

STUDENTS PERFORM EXTRACURRICULAR first-person historical presentations for the purpose of creating and presenting first-person historical characters in relationship to their geographic community. Students use this method to combine historical context with the human dimension of building a sense of community. Many times teachers ignore or skip community studies because of a mistaken view that the content is provincial or relatively unimportant. The great importance of content in local studies helps students to learn in context with their community. Students use drama to interpret historical content for an audience in the community. Students research, prepare, and connect with their community; as a result the students learn to value public speaking and service, as well as their community.

RATIONALE

Students study social studies in order to learn to become good citizens in a democratic republic. The study of citizenship education has captivated scholars for many years (Davies, Gregory, & Riley, 1999; Leming, Ellington, & Schug, 2006; Rubin & Giarelli, 2006). Spanning the Atlantic from Britain to the United States, citizenship is a crucial topic for educators' interest in helping students relate to their community. Citizens find common ground when they come together to form a community. Students and adults can work together on common projects to enrich their lives and make contributions to one another.

> What . . . distinguishes the citizen empowerment of this era is that it is not a special need of a special group of activists, say, or big-shot public figures. Rather, the Americans we talk with understand that the need to contribute to that which is beyond ourselves—maybe even beyond our lifetimes—is a need that resides in almost all of us. (Lappe' & DuBois, 1994, p. 301)

Empowered citizens feel ownership in their democracy and want to make contributions; in the past citizenship left people out of the political process, but over time more people have attained the right of participation. The brilliant quality of democratic citizenship is that even when counterattacked it retains the ability to redefine itself to allow more people to enter into participation (Brosio, 2000; Wyness, 2006; Yinger, 2005). People gain representation through citizenship, and as people become involved they contribute and pass on gifts to others. At the local level students see participation in communities as a type of political involvement that connects themselves and how they make contributions.

> Students find involvement within their community.
> The community is a fundamental and irreplaceable part of the good life for human beings and full participation in community life is important for experiencing this good life; further, the self is "embedded" in and partly constituted by communal commitments and values that are not always objects of choice. (Arthur, 2000, p. 134)

In Britain the Labor Party supports the ideals of communitarianism as that community which ties improvement to academic life; moreover, the interaction between the community and the individual cannot be overemphasized. With individualistic excesses tempered by consideration of the community interests, educators valued the ideals of community. The faculty of Dewey's lab school sought to stimulate these connections forming a community to support students from different backgrounds and help them to find a home at school (Enright, Schaefer, Schaefer, & Schaefer, 2008; Tanner, 1997). The students then coalesced as a community of learners who learned and worked together while supporting one another. Students worked with their community to explore what was immediate and real. In addition many students and teachers talked about community, neighborhoods, and cities in their elementary social studies curriculum, but real community building needs to travel from the classroom, through the school, and into the world (Bell & Henning, 2007; Buendia, Meacham, & Noffke, 2000; Gonzales, Riedel, Williamson, Avery, Sullivan, & Bos, 2004; Thompson, 2006). Students need to act in their community to both improve and support it. The community members need to see their children in a positive light by working with them and celebrating their accomplishments. The community members need to send the message that the community both values and includes the students.

When students present first-person historical presentations, they use drama methods to communicate historical content to an audience. They use elaborate communication to transfer information to their audiences. Students use drama while they learn social studies, and Fines and Verrier (1974; McGuire & Cole, 2005) found that fifth grade students benefited when they learned content. They encouraged students to make democratic decision-making within an informed community and to see the implications of those decisions for the classroom members. Another set of British researchers looked at the effects of drama on thinking skills. Golan and Hendy (1993; Stoskopf, 2001) found that not only did students learn content from the British national curriculum, but the students also increased their test scores of intellectual thinking and reasoning skills on Britain's national testing instrument. Using dramatic methods in social studies made a valuable contribution not only to the development of student creativity but also to thinking skills. Students considered their position and the positions they encountered from other characters. Students need to have investment, group ownership, and some degree of control or stake in their learning, and Taylor (1995, 1998; Meden, 1999) found that students could reflect, learn from the process of performing drama,

and examine multiple perspectives. Students viewed multiple perspectives from first-person historical presentation and considered
decision-making by viewing a problem from other perspectives. As
a class, community students practiced their thinking skills as they
considered the social studies as both thinking and learning. Students placed their feelings and expression into the work while also
connecting emotionally with it.

A classroom could work with content as remote as ancient history and connect the community of the past to the daily community life of present students. Morris (1998, 2001; Guerrero, 2007;
Kelin, 2005) found seventh-grade students built a democratic community while they learned social studies and used drama. Students
collaborated and made decisions to help the members of the class
learn content and skills while making connections between different times, places, and present situations. Students also spent time
out of school working with drama and establishing connections
to the past. Students used drama beyond school to continue their
education for recreational purposes. Morris (2000) found that
students used extracurricular social studies enrichment that contained drama to develop connections with their community. Students experienced their community through study travel, research
skills, reenactment, and sharing information. Students learned to
be contributing citizens within their community when they made
decisions, improved their thinking skills, connected with problems,
collaborated, and developed connections with their community.
When teachers use drama in social studies, they encourage students to make connections with the community, but when they use
the form of first-person historical presentations do they also make
connections to the community?

THE PROCESS

The community of Hope started as a Moravian colony when settlers
came from Bethlehem, Pennsylvania, and Salem, North Carolina,
to establish a settlement in Indiana similar to the pattern of Old
Salem, North Carolina. Hope had a rich historical setting and a

long tradition of supporting and encouraging heritage preservation activities. Many of the residents had family connections in the town dating back to the establishment of the community in the early 1800s. The founding residents established a girl's seminary early in the town's existence, and education remained important to the community members. The small town of Hope, Indiana, in a rural setting has one junior/senior high school building located next to one upper elementary school, which houses the third through sixth grades. While many of the long-time residents shared common ancestors, still others held church or social bonds; the low taxes and available land near major urban areas encouraged transient population growth in low-income apartments and low-cost housing. Students representing rural poverty and single parent homes filled the classrooms of this community. The rich history of the small town suggested that there might be particularly strong interest in preserving the heritage of the town. The school board members are very proud that their two townships remain unconsolidated into the much larger county school system that includes a small city.

The community had informally recognized these adolescents participating in an extracurricular endeavor as outstanding representatives of the town. The seventeen sixth-, seventh-, and eighth-grade students attending Hope Junior/Senior High worked with a local elementary school teacher, Barbara Johnson, to present first-person historical presentations for third-grade students who went on a one-day walking tour of their town history. The third-grade students learned about their town as part of their third-grade social studies curriculum that focused on their community, and they use the National Council for the Social Studies standards (1994) [see appendix II]:

II. Time, Continuity, and Change
III. People, Places, and Environments
V. Individuals, Groups, and Institutions
VII. Production, Distribution, and Consumption

In the program, students chose a person from history whom they believed made a contribution to their town. Over a two-week period students examined as many biographies, autobiographies, primary sources, settings, and time period descriptions as possible in order to really become their character. Students learned about technique, believability, resources, contextualizing their character, and costuming. The students found appropriate costumes, props, and primary sources for their characters. They performed their presentations in the local cemetery next to their character's grave and told how their lives changed the town.

These students volunteered, developed a long-term interest in performing their characters, and did this as an extracurricular activity. They may have had a special affinity with living in this particular small town that students in a large urban area may not have. However, the experience does tell how one group of students dealt with forming connections through their community, and how those students used first-person historical presentations to interpret that experience. Students used local studies to connect with their community in this one particular situation. The Cemetery Walk program was an extracurricular activity for the student participants. There was no class participation, and no student received a grade or extra credit for the project. Mrs. Johnson, a local teacher, worked with her former third-grade students who are middle-school historical presenters. She depended upon the relations with her past students, the proximity of the former students, her role as a local historian, and her role in the community to entice students to participate. She helped them to identify a character they wanted to depict, to find research materials, write a script, and practice their parts. She arranged release time for the students to miss class to do this presentation during a school day, transportation for the students, and a cooler of drinks after the presentation. Once the students knew their parts, she worked to find multiple venues where they could perform their presentations.

Through guests, examples, modeling, and group discussions, Mrs. Johnson introduced a group of former students to first-person historical presentations during their sixth-grade year; these students continued to interpret and develop their chosen characters for a total of three years. Other students joined the original group over the years; all of them chose characters representative of their community's history. Students interpreted and presented their characters in a local cemetery (Bigelow, 1995; Lindquist, 1995; Michels & Maxwell, 2006; Morris, 2002; Percoco, 1998), where they performed before Mrs. Johnson's current third-grade students. During a daylong walk these elementary students learned about their community and met people who had made an impact on their community while seeing the character's grave in the town cemetery. The students volunteered to do this research with their former teacher as an extracurricular project. They performed for local festivals and for third-grade students, as well as for their class.

STUDENT EXPERIENCES

Students researched within the community, prepared their scripts, and presented their program. In addition to the Moravian Church opening their records to the students, the students used multiple community sources, including traditional library sources, historical society photos, private collections, the local history museum, community newspapers, and historic sites. The junior high school students engaged in oral history with local residents and consulted local residents to find out about their characters. Many of the students talked to relatives or former acquaintances of the characters; some students even lived on the same or adjacent land. Since many of the children who lived in the community had family connections to many present and past residents of the town, some students possessed family memorabilia from these people. "We went to the library and got information off of the Internet and wrote up our papers" (Cleo). As a result of their research, students typed one-page scripts to present to their audience. The community supported these inquiries through the original compilation of the materials and through the selection of locally eminent people. "We researched. Ms. Johnson took us to the library and we looked through books. And then we went to the cemetery. We just picked out somebody that we though[t] I could use. And we just researched her" (Blair). Students felt supported in their selection, creation, and presentation of characters for first-person presentations, and they

used a variety of sources to find the information that they needed
to present their character effectively to their audience.

Moreover, in order to convincingly portray their character,
students fielded questions from the audience. They found that the
events during the cemetery walk broadened their experience and
that the experience propelled them into the future. The students
found that they benefited from the questions generated from the
members of the audience. "Some of them can recall the people and
they will ask us questions and if we don't know they will tell us and
give us more ideas of what we are doing" (Cleo). The community
members provided information to the students from their memories
of the person whom the students presented. In turn the students
recognized and appreciated the knowledge of the senior members
of the community. "When the first time we did it with the older
[people] and our parents, they asked us questions. They would help
us, 'cause a lot of the older people, they've known a lot about it and
so they kind of helped us with more details" (Mindy). The senior
members of the community helped the students by fleshing out
their presentations with accounts of their childhood in town and
stories of people they knew. Students are evaluated by the community members and elders who pass judgment on verbal communication skills, historical accuracy, and depth of student knowledge.
The community members are not shy about offering suggestions or
comments prior to presentations to elementary students. In addition, students found encouragement, support, and direction from
teachers, parents, and community members.

Students believed that they performed a service for the community. Many social studies philosophers and researchers have
encouraged the teaching of social studies at every age to encourage
citizens to improve democracy. These writers urged students in
social studies to become active participants within their communities (Barr, Barth, & Shermis, 1978; Brophy & Van Sledright, 1997;
Engle & Ochoa, 1988; Goodman, 1992; Hahn, 1998; Koralek
& Mindes, 2006; Morris, 2007; Parker, 1997; Ross, 1997; Sehr,
1997; Wade, 1998). These students explored ideas and impacted
the community, they realized the limits of personnel in the community, and they provided an important service that supported the

members of the town. They realized that they worked with an audience that was motivated to learn about what they had to share. "Our
audiences are from Hope too, and they are interested to learn about
Hope's past and history" (Joe). The students realized that many
people in the community wanted to know more about their past
and that those people depended on the students to provide that
information. Students felt a sense of fulfillment when they realized
that they provided a valuable service that was of great meaning to
their community, and that they performed work usually expected
from more mature members of the community.

> It's always important to learn new things, and people do learn a
> lot I think. They try to absorb as much as they can out of what
> you say and that makes it important to use, because we know that
> these people who come there are learning something and you are
> making a difference to them. (Stuart)

Students knew that their contributions were important, that they
impacted their audience, and that in a democracy citizens need to
know that they can make a difference in their community. Students
knew that as citizens they performed a service for the others in their
community, and that they initiated positive change in their town.
Students actively participated to help the audience members learn
about their past.

Students also formed connections with the people of their
community. Students used the method of first-person presentation
and interpreted the town of Hope, defined the people who lived
there in the past, and provided meaning for the inhabitants of today. "People need to know about where they live and what they're
hearing about" (Mindy). Students provided knowledge that helped
the people in their community to get a sense of their community.
Students expressed pride in their neighbors and shared their knowledge about their pride with others.

> If we're ever asked anything about our community then we can be
> proud we did that and we can understand what our community is
> and who we are. If anyone ever asks me any question about the
> Moravian Church, we know there is Reverend Holland, his wife,

and then you can tell them about the female seminary. There were a lot of firsts in Hope that nobody ever knew about, and we're really proud of that . . . If anybody ever asks about it then we can know the background on it; . . . we can step up and say, "Hey, I know what happened then, because I did some research on it." It makes you feel really good about letting other people know, about your town, it makes you really proud. (Missy)

Students were proud of their town, proud of their role in interpreting the town, and proud of how they defined the way community members fit into the history of the town of Hope. The students acted as agents of investigation, communication, and dissemination. The students established connections with the people in the town when they knew who these people were and why they were important.

Students realized that their audience felt good about the experience and that the community validated their work. They reported eye contact and body language as response indicators for the students, and the students realized that they had contributed to the community members' enjoyment.

I could tell the people who are watching, how they reacted if they had a smile on their face and you could tell that they were thinking about something. It makes you feel . . . I did something good. That's how I think you oughta feel about it. The teacher and the third graders are all smiling when everybody's out there on the field. (Reba)

Students thought that they should have positive feelings about their community, and that participants should feel good when learning about the community. They liked the fact that they had done something positive for the community. Students determined from the verbal expressions of thanks and additional questions asked of them that the audience was interested and appreciative of their work.

The first time we did it, we had a real[ly] good response. A lot of people thanked us and though[t] it was a real[ly] neat idea, 'cause no one's ever heard of a stroll into the past . . . in the cemetery. I think they responded to it real[ly] well. At the end they asked us questions, and I think they enjoyed it. They told us they enjoyed it, so. One year my parents took a video camera and taped us, so we got to see how we did. (Tara)

Tara's parents celebrated her contribution when they filmed her presentation, and the students retrospectively viewed their presentations. Community validation helped students realize how important this project was to Hope's citizens. Students helped their audience to feel good about their program, and the audience reciprocated by helping the students to know the value of their work.

Student Meanings

These findings reflected three ideas; first was the phenomena, or what was the nature of this event. A student used a metaphor of a memoir to describe this cemetery walk as if it were a thing like a yearbook. "It's a memoir about where I live, and you can relate to some of the stuff that happens and understand it" (Joe). The students place the metaphor in the context of a geographical place with the context of understanding as a part of this experience in the understanding of the value to the community. "The older people, they are surprised that we know this much, and they're glad that we learned of important people in history that are from Hope. And they're surprised with all the research we've done and everything we do know about this guy" (Ethan). The students understood that the older generations of the community were grateful that the students remembered the past and wanted to recall it. The students understood the expectations the senior members have of them for taking leadership in the preservation of the past. "People expect things out of you" (Jeremy). Jeremy expressed a sense of responsibility to the community and a clear sense of obligation to the community members. Further the students expressed personal connections that they feel to people from the past. "On the barn at the house that was his, there's a picture of a hog, and I never knew what any of that was. And there's some drawings and stuff at our old house that we had in the basement there was writing on the wall, and in the barn on the wall it had a lot of hogs' names and I didn't know what they were.

But when I started doing this I learned that those were all animals that he had" (Ethan). Ethan documented the life of a prize-winning hog farmer and found connections from the actual site where the farmer and Ethan once lived. The sense of place in using the built environment was very important in how the student explored and interpreted the past. "I got interested in him because I live in his old house" (Stuart). Stuart had an even more personal connection to place, which resulted from inhabiting the former house of his character. The phenomenon of the cemetery walk consisted of an interaction between value to the community and personal connection between the student and their characters. The students found inspiration from an interaction between the two that helped the students to find this cemetery walk meaningful.

Students found that the cemetery walk event was particularly meaningful to their life. Some students pointed to the public speaking experience that the event provided. "It also helps for when we talk in front of people for our public speaking" (Jeremy). Students said they improved their public speaking ability, they grew in presentation skills, and they reduced their anxiety level. Students especially expressed their abilities of speaking in front of groups as being strengthened by this experience. "It's kind of like acting . . . It kind of helped me get over my fear of getting in front of people" (Craig). Blair used the experience to overcome inhibitions that she had in presenting information to groups of people. "I think it helps my speech skills, speaking in front of people because before I used to look down at the floor, now I can look around and look everybody in the eyes. I am not scared anymore" (Blair). When students saw themselves as part of a community, it was no longer as anxiety-producing as when people were outside a group. Students anticipated taking this experience with a group that they became comfortable with and transferring their experiences to other groups. "It taught me, I can speak better in front of people now, 'cause by standing there and talking in front of many large groups of people some of my fears are over, it prepares me for talking in front of other people" (Ethan). Students, as part of the community, did not need to feel intimidated or feel excluded by it. Students recognized the benefit of enhanced presentation skills as a positive benefit of their participation in this program. They looked for opportunities to transfer their knowledge to future experiences with other groups of people, and students learned to speak in public forums to improve their skills. Students said that this experience prepared them for the future.

Students also saw the potential for being in front of people as excellent preparation for future situations whether in college, high school, work, or in the community. Jeremy found the experience beneficial because it transferred immediately to his plans for the future. "In college if we have to give a speech . . . this can help us on our speech and being in front of people" (Jeremy). Students saw that the method helped them achieve their future vocation. If social studies should prepare students for leadership positions, this was a good experience for the students. Students practiced speaking before groups of people—a leadership role they will fill many times. The students who remain in the community will need to speak about many issues from school board meetings to organizing youth groups. The students saw vocational implications in future drama performance jobs. "Yes as far as performing in front of an audience, some day I want to be an actor so this really helps me to go out in front of crowds" (Todd). Todd saw direct vocational benefits from this type of experience. Students saw immediate connections to their future. They could easily justify this experience as having applications to their future skills or careers.

For these students, learning history was important. Students pointed to the interactive nature of the experience. The students learned history in a mentor and mentored fashion. While the students did read books, the reading was different from the traditional school text assignment."I think it is easy for people to learn because it is person to person and you don't have to read it out of books. And I think that I have learned a lot from doing it myself instead of just reading it out of a book" (Blair). The aspect of heritage, or the spirit of place, was important to the students. "It was really interesting to learn[ing] the heritage of our town 'cause we're going to be living here a lot longer, and some of us might raise a family here and it would be kinda interesting to tell them how we started . . . People think history class is boring but doing it this way makes it a lot more interesting and fun" (Mindy). The students realized that their connection to family and place made this information important, and their continuity in place and lineage connected them to their heritage. The students see lineage and place as being connected in their heritage. "I just think it's important that the community can know so much about this, and I think that we should know more about our past so then we can pass that on to others, to our next generation. A lot of people at Heritage Days actually learned a lot. . . It's important that they know who these people are" (Reba). For the students this lineage is meritorious to pass on to the following generations. Moreover, the students had direct experience where they actively participated in this learning event. The students identified this style of teaching and learning as being hands on. "It is . . . [fun] when it is hands on instead of sitting in school with the teacher telling you stuff. With hands on it is more interesting" (Craig). The students liked being active learners and directing their own research projects; they became a source of knowledge rather than merely a receiver of knowledge. The students also liked the assessments in the form of presentations for a real audience. "It's fun, 'cause it's kinda tying history in our town, and English and grammar skills into one thing, and I think that's a really good hands-on project" (Missy). They saw the application of knowledge as requiring interdisciplinary communication skills. They combined social studies disciplines, social studies knowledge and skills, and other disciplines outside of social studies with social studies knowledge. The students found meaning in this program through the phenomenon of the cemetery walk, the participation in the event, and the opportunity to learn history.

CONCLUSIONS

Because the students considered themselves to be included in the community as valued members of the town, the young people truly became peers who shared the wisdom and knowledge of the past with others. The students received immediate positive feedback from the community members who saw the students' performance.

The older people, they are surprised that we know this much and they're glad that we learned of the important people in history that are from Hope. And they're surprised with all the research we've done and everything we know about this guy. (Ethan)

The people of the town demonstrated their pleasure at the work done by the students who interpreted the past. Behaviors that the community members exhibited included supportive questioning, reassuring, establishing a common link with the person, or providing additional information to the students.

The older people asked us questions [and] tried to make us feel better about what we were doing so we didn't feel quite as scared. They helped us out, and they would ask a lot of questions about them. Or they would tell us about them, [things] that we may not have mentioned[, or] that they knew the person. (Blair)

The community members paid attention to the students and students appreciated this positive attention. The young people served as role models for the community exemplifying the potential of young people. The presentations also served as a rite of passage metaphorically initiating the young people into the community with the requisite knowledge, skills, values, and participation needed for inclusion.

This experience reflected student ownership of the learning process. What attracted students to this program was the ability to choose their own character, and develop it in a way that was reflective of their personality and learning styles. The meetings offered guidance and feedback, but the vast majority of study and preparation was independent. The program also offered both intrinsic and extrinsic rewards. The research and preparation required for each of these characters were impressive to the students, and intrinsically, students felt a sense of accomplishment as they created and refined their character. While Mrs. Johnson coached and encouraged the students, there were no grades, and no real reward until the end. The extrinsic reward did happen. For those students who persevered, the applause after a performance in front of the community was both attractive and rewarding.

There may be some implications for social studies educators in these results. Using first-person historical characters may be an appropriate strategy for student learning because it requires students to become active participants and decision-makers in their education. Students do not remain passive; they must actively engage in the experience. Results also indicate the potential for intrinsic motivation in such a project or other projects of a student's choosing. It is their project, and they make the most of it.

THOUGHT QUESTIONS

1. How did you connect with your community?
2. How could this project be applied to an urban or suburban class?
3. How can communities recognize the meaningful accomplishments of young people?
4. Have you ever participated in a cross-grade project?
   a. Do you remember any thoughts or feelings about it?
5. Could this project be replicated in an urban or suburban area?
   a. Why or why not?
6. How did you form connections to your community?
   a. What relationship did you have to the elders of your community?

REFERENCES

Arthur, J. (2000). *Schools and community: The communitarian agenda in education*. New York: Falmer.

Barr, R., Barth, J., & Shermis, S. (1978). *The nature of the social studies*. Palm Springs, CA: ETC Publications.

Bell, D., & Henning, M. B. (2007). DeKalb County, Illinois: A local history project for second graders. *Social Studies and the Young Learner, 19*(3), 7-11.

Blair (2001). Interview by author. Hope, IN, 10 May.

Bigelow, B. (1995). Show, don't tell: Role plays and social imagination. In M. Burke-Hengen & T. Gillespie (Eds.), *Building community: Social studies in the middle school years* (pp. 73–90). Portsmouth, NH: Heinemann.

Brophy, B., & Van Sledright, B. (1997). *Teaching and learning history in elementary schools.* New York: Teachers College Press.

Brosio, R. A. (2000). *Philosophical scaffolding for the construction of critical democratic education.* New York: Lang.

Buendia, E., Meacham, S., & Noffke, S. E. (2000). Community, displacement, and inquiry: Living social justice in a social studies methods course. In D. W. Hursh & E. W. Ross (Eds.), *Democratic social education: Social studies for social change* (pp. 165–188). New York: Falmer.

Cleo (2001). Interview by author. Hope, IN, 11 May.

Craig (2001). Interview by author. Hope, IN, 11 May.

Davies, I., Gregory, I., & Riley, S. C. (1999). *Good citizenship and educational provision.* New York: Falmer.

Engle, S. H., & Ochoa, A. S. (1988). *Education for democratic citizenship: Decision making in the social studies.* New York: Teachers College Press.

Enright, M. S., Schaefer, L. V., Schaefer, P. S., & Schaefer, K. A. (2008). Building a just adolescent community. *Montessori Life: A publication of the American Montessori Society, 20*(1), 36–42.

Ethan (2001). Interview by author. Hope, IN, 10 May.

Fines, J., & Verrier, R. (1974). *The drama of history: An experiment in cooperative teaching.* London: New University Education.

Golan, P,. & Hendy, L. (1993). 'It's not just fun, it works!' Developing children's historical thinking through drama. *The Curriculum Journal, 4*(3) 363–384.

Goodman, J. (1992). *Elementary schooling for critical democracy.* Albany: State University of New York Press.

Gonzales, M. H., Riedel, E., Williamson, I., Avery, P. G., Sullivan, J. L., & Bos, A. (2004). Variations of citizenship education: A content analysis of rights, obligations, and participation concepts in high school civic textbooks. *Theory and Research in Social Education, 32*(3), 301–325.

Guerrero, K. (2007). A world bazaar: Learning about community, geography, and economics. *Social Studies and the Young Learner, 19*(4), 4–6.

Hahn, C. L. (1998). *Becoming political: Comparative perspectives on citizenship education.* Albany: State University of New York Press.

Jeremy (2001). Interview by author. Hope, IN, 12 May.

Joe (2001). Interview by author. Hope, IN, 10 May.

Kelin, D. A., II. (2005). Voyages of discovery: Experiencing the emotions of history. *Social Studies and the Young Learner, 18*(1), 7–10.

Koralek, D., & Mindes, G. (2006). *Spotlight on young children and social studies.* Washington, D.C.: National Association for the Education of Young Children.

Lappe', F. M., & DuBois, P. M. (1994). *The quickening of America: Rebuilding our nation, remaking our lives.* San Francisco: Jossey-Bass.

Leming, J. S., Ellington, L., & Schug, M. (2006). The state of social studies: A national random survey of elementary and middle school social studies teachers. *Social Education, 70*(5), 322–327.

Lindquist, T. (1995). *Seeing the whole through social studies.* Portsmouth, NH: Heinemann.

McGuire, M. E., & Cole, B. (2005). Using Storypath to give young learners a fair start. *Social Studies and the Young Learner, 18*(2), 20–23.

Meden, M. (1999). Classroom success stories: History comes alive in the classroom. *Social Studies, 90*(5), 237–238.

Michels, B. J., & Maxwell, D. K. (2006). An after-school program for interpreting local history. *TechTrends: Linking Research and Practice to Improve Learning, 50*(2), 62–66.

Mindy (2001). Interview by author. Hope, IN, 13 May.

Missy (2001). Interview by author. Hope, IN, 11 May.

Morris, R. V. (2007). Social studies around the blacksmith's forge: Interdisciplinary teaching and learning. *Social Studies, 98*(3), 99–104.

———. (2002). Middle school first-person presentations and connection to the community. *Research in Middle Level Education Online, 26*(1), http://www.nmsa.org/.

———. (2001). How teachers can conduct historical reenactments in their own schools. *Childhood Education, 77*(4), 196–203.

———. (2000). The history walk: Integrated multi-age learning. *Gifted Child Today, 23*(4), 22–27, 53.

———. (1998). Common threads: How to translate best practices into teaching. *Journal of Social Studies Research, 22*(2), 11–18.

National Council for the Social Studies. (1994). *Expectations of excellence: Curriculum standards for social studies.* Washington, D.C.: Author.

Parker, W. C. (1997). *Educating the democratic mind.* Albany: State University of New York Press.

Percoco, J. A. (1998). *A passion for the past: Creative teaching of U.S. history.* Portsmouth, NH: Heinemann.

Reba (2001). Interview by author. Hope, IN, 10 May.

Ross, E. W. (1997). *The social studies curriculum: Purposes, problems, and possibilities.* Albany: State University of New York Press.

Rubin, B. C., & Giarelli, J. M. (Eds.) (2006). *Civic education for diverse citizens in global times: Rethinking theory and practice*. Mahway, NJ: Lawrence Erlbaum Associates.

Sehr, D. T. (1997). *Education for public democracy*. Albany: State University of New York Press.

Stoskopf, A. (2001). Reviving Clio: Inspired history teaching and learning (without high-stakes tests). *Phi Delta Kappan*, 9(4), 468–473.

Stuart (2001). Interview by author. Hope, IN, 12 May.

Tara (2001). Interview by author. Hope, IN, 14 May.

Tanner, L. N. (1997). *Dewey's laboratory school: Lessons for today*. New York: Teachers College Press.

Taylor, P. (1998). *Redcoats and patriots: Reflective practice in drama and social studies*. Portsmouth, NH: Heinemann.

———. (1995). Our adventure of experiencing: Reflective practice and drama research. *Youth Theatre Journal*, 9, 31–52.

Thomson, P. (2006). Miners, diggers, ferals and show-men: School-community projects that affirm and unsettle identities and place? *British Journal of Sociology of Education*, 27(1), 81–96.

Todd (2001). Interview by author. Hope, IN, 10 May.

Wade, R. (1998). *Community service-learning: A guide to including service in the public school curriculum*. Albany: State University of New York Press.

Wyness, M. (2006). Children, young people and civic participation: Regulation and local diversity. *Educational Review*, 58(2), 209–218.

Yinger, R. J. (2005). The promise of education. *Journal of Education for Teaching*, 31(4), 307–310.

Chapter Seven

──────────○──────────

Third and Seventh Grade Texas History Walk[1]

SEVENTH- AND THIRD-GRADE STUDENTS helped each other learn what life was like in the 1870s on the Texas frontier. The Texas History Walk at All Saints School allowed third-grade students to meet characters from the past—these were the inhabitants of the land that the students presently occupy. The people of the 1870s were very diverse, and the conflicts between these people determined who held power for the next one hundred years. The struggle was between those who ranged the land and those who settled it, or as they saw it, improved it. Students got to work together across grade levels to learn more about the interaction between people, and together they got to explore the diversity of the people who now live together in peace rather than in conflict on this land. The Texas History Walk allowed third-grade people to walk to the simulated camps of many different people, where the students got to talk with them, found out why they were present, and discovered what they might trade with them.

RATIONALE

Since its inception social studies has always been interdisciplinary using content from a variety of disciplines. In this program the content came from the social science disciplines of economics,

93

geography, and the subject of history. The interdisciplinary nature of the program interwove the themes of "Production, Distribution, and Consumption" from the National Council for the Social Studies standards (1994) with the related standards of "People, Places, and Environments" and "Time, Continuity, and Change" (Brophy & VanSledright, 1997; Gandy, 2007; Millward, 2007; Morris, 2007; Stevens & Starkey, 2007) [see appendix II]. Students therefore could understand the interrelated qualities of the social studies disciplines. Students used these standards contained in drama while in situations that reenacted a particular moment. Researchers find drama to be an effective method of integrating social studies materials (Fines & Verrier, 1974; Goalen & Hendy, 1993; Kelin, 2005; Morris, 1998; Peterson, 2004). Student immersion in a time period allows them the opportunity to explore issues and ideas from a specific time. These specific students worked with a re-creation of a time period to learn content from multiple disciplines as students worked to find out about their lives in the re-creation of time and place. Students, immersed in content, got to experience a deep understanding of the Southwest.

Students saw that the age of the cowboys, unlike that shown by the media, consisted of many different groups and people. Representatives of these groups coexisted on the frontier either as allies or enemies (Banks, 1991; Marri, 2005). Students need to learn to coexist in a multiethnic democracy and world. People make up their community, and their interests will either be in common or, if in conflict, they must learn to compromise. Students who see historic, economic, and geographic connections or animosity need to apply that information to present-day situations. Students see multiple groups of people in social studies that are both inclusive and realistic.

Each grade contributed to the other as the seventh- and third-grade students worked together. The seventh-grade students found out more about supply and demand as well as marketing or by observing the pioneer third-grade students who were hesitant to part with their savings (NCEE, 1997). The third-grade students learned about the different reasons why people arrived, departed, or remained on the frontier. While each group of students felt that they were doing something or providing a service for the others, they also realized that they were learning and growing from the experience. Seventh-grade students took on leadership roles in interpreting the site for younger students while younger students completed the trading process. The students traded with one another and practiced economics rather than merely listening to discussions about it.

PROCEDURES

Third-grade students prepared for the day by reading about Laura Ingalls Wilder as a pioneer figure of the time. Students found more information about Laura and her family from the Internet, which continued where the books ended. The teacher, Mrs. Lance, provided the students with videos about Mrs. Wilder, the period of time, and an actual interview with her. The students also experienced first-person presentations performed by teachers from the university elementary social studies method class. Students sampled food typical of the Victorian Age and engaged in some of the crafts and jobs from Mrs. Wilder's life. The students identified with an individual; Mrs. Wilder then transferred that knowledge of a person to a different place within the same time period.

Mrs. McNeely introduced the seventh-grade students to the different possible groups that they could represent; students formed groups by selecting roles. To research and write about local and state figures the students picked the major characters and found where they lived and what they did. Students went to the local university and worked with the special collections library staff; students from the university middle-school social studies methods class helped the seventh-grade students learn more about primary sources. Students used at least five secondary sources from the comprehensive classroom collection of state and local history, wrote note and bibliography cards, and when they were ready to pool their resources, the groups used folders to organize their materials. First students scripted their character; next they worked on interactions between their characters; they then worked on the interaction between their character and their audience; and finally they made their presentation appear to be impromptu. The scripts needed to be conversational in nature lest the event sound like three separate mannequins speaking when they performed their presentations for one another. Students fielded questions in character so they knew the information thoroughly, rather than having it memorized. Third-grade students interrupted the seventh graders with questions so the seventh-grade students had to be able to think on their feet in order to respond with appropriate answers.

Students found authentic items that complemented their presentations and attracted student interest to their topic. They went to great lengths to find artifacts and costuming that were appropriate for their situation and characterization. In order to get ideas they looked at museum collections, books on period clothing and antiques, old pictures, and reproductions (Morris, 2000). To manage storage and retrieval, students kept the props in a central location and inconspicuously tagged many of the artifacts. The students borrowed a large number of props to use in the events; they secured these props from relatives, county museums, and local ranches. Each group stored their props in the large plastic prop boxes labeled for their group; at the end of the event, students sorted and cleaned everything for storage in preparation for next year's presentation.

Seventh-grade students manipulated their environment to make the site believable to the third-grade students. Students worked to develop sets; on one location they constructed a dugout—a structure buried into the side of the canyon with only the front and roof exposed. Students spent a Saturday volunteering by cutting trees at Mrs. McNeely's ranch; the lumber was brought to the school where the students unloaded it. The students worked hard to create an effective setting by using this lumber to construct a brush arbor for the buffalo hunters. Third-grade students imagined the rest of the setting after the seventh-grade students established the historic mood.

Students engaged in a variety of activities that stimulated their multiple senses; they gained these experiences through recreation and leisure as well. The students gave the buffalo chips in the fire rings a wary glance—some ideas do not transfer easily to the twenty-first century. While these experiences were somewhat foreign to the students, the students were able to relate their experiences to their present life and imagined how that experience occurred in the past. To get the seventh-grade students ready for this history walk, preparatory experiences gave students events similar to those their characters might have experienced in the 1870s, whether it was eating buffalo steaks or heating a branding iron in an open fire. These types of direct experiences helped students to understand more about the life and time of the people they were impersonating.

Mrs. McNeely used class time to help students learn more about the time period. Many resource people came into the classroom as guests to share their knowledge and experiences. Resource people brought their memories, contemporary experience, and artifacts to share with the students. Mrs. McNeely invited a local songwriter and poet to talk and sing about the events of local figures from the 1870s, and he told of how he did his research using family and community resources. Through poetry and music, the artist showed how to share both mood and ideas with the audience through poems, delivery, and song. Many other resource people shared information, including a representative from a local county museum, the granddaughter of an early settler, the Texas Rangers, a reenactment group depicting the 4th Cavalry, and a consultant procured to act as a drama conductor. The drama conductor worked with the students to help them communicate their ideas to the audience effectively.

The dress rehearsal occurred the Saturday before the actual Texas History Walk, and the seventh-grade students set the stage by putting up a teepee and getting their area ready. The students had lunch, got into their costumes, and then gave their presentations for their parents, who served as the audience for the dress rehearsal. This was a good opportunity to practice with a spontaneous and friendly audience. The experience with fielding questions helped students get ready for the third-grade students who would arrive in just a few days. This social studies experience was both meaningful to the students and easily assessed by everyone who witnessed the students' elaborate communication skills. In addition the third-grade students demonstrated their accomplishments through successful trading. The students created a chart story describing the experiences they had, and each student made an exchange map showing what they got and what they gave. The public audience evaluated the seventh-grade students by examining their story, questioning their details, and critiquing the accuracy of the students.

EXAMPLE

On the day of the Texas History Walk, four rotations began the three-hour program—two rotations in the morning and two in the afternoon. Ten groups of third-grade students made the rounds between each station at fifteen-minute intervals while seventh-grade students made their presentations. The rotations allowed for up to four hundred people to come through the Texas History Walk if groups of ten participated. Students started at each station; they did not need to start at any particular place, but the rotations moved in a clockwise order. The students heard a triangle ring when it was time to move to the next station.

The day of the living history walk culminated when the students performed their presentations, and the third-grade students greeted them as if they were fellow settlers in the Southwest. The third-grade students dressed up in cowboy attire and ate lunch at a chuck wagon from a local ranch before or after going on the living history trail. Students from the lower school bought into the day by picking a ma, pa, brothers, sisters, and extended relations for their group that had come from the eastern part of the state and were moving west. It would have been very odd for settlers to be separated from their wagon. They explained the loss of their wagon when crossing the river in a flood, and they constantly watched for Indians who viewed them as trespassers. This family group moved together for the next hour, and they played their individual and group roles as they traveled. The Cavalry, Buffalo Soldiers, and Texas Rangers all tried to find the Indians.

These different groups allowed students to see a variety of people living together in harmony or in tension with one another.

African-American Buffalo Soldiers, Anglo settlers, Hispanic Pastores and Comancheros, and Native American Comanches all lived there before towns, settlements, and cities were established. The presentations included four parts: the introduction of the character; context of the character including work, job, and historical significance; explanation of props; and trading. The third-grade students met Susanna Dickinson who was surrounded by trunks and quilts; the Pastores who camped next to their sheepfold; Col. MacKenzie's 4th Cavalry camp that included a tent, horse, and campfire; the Comancheros who camped around their large solid wheeled trade wagon that was heaped high with trade goods for the Comanches who would buy their merchandise; and the Buffalo Soldier's camp that included a tent and camp fire. Paris Cox, the first settler in the county, was on a picnic with his relatives with quilts, baskets, and canned food. The buffalo hunter's camp included a student-constructed brush arbor, bones, buffalo skins, and hides. At the Texas Ranger Camp younger students saw the rangers with their horse and tent, and Quanah Parker received strangers at his teepee complete with travois and fire pit with a buffalo stomach. Col. Goodnight met guests while surrounded by chickens, branding irons, and a chuck wagon. Cox and Goodnight represented residents and the changes those people brought to the living pattern compared to other more migratory inhabitants. All of these people on the high plains of west Texas made contributions and had an impact on each other through their lives and their stories.

When third-grade students entered the area, they needed resources so that they could trade, and they got an overview as to what they might be able to do with these resources. Students talked about the role of government in providing state employees and federal troops to keep an uneasy peace; the students worked with a mixed barter and cash economy and made choices as to what to purchase and under what circumstances. Young students got beads, a Bible, rabbit skins, candles, and $100 in 1870 scrip to trade with the different people they met along the journey. At the first stop they met a family that was moving back east; they traded for cornmeal and soap. When they met the Pastores, they traded for cheese and wool. At the cavalry encampment they got hardtack. The

Comancheros ransomed the white captives from the Comanches with trade goods, and the Buffalo Soldiers shared their rations of coffee and salt pork with the students. At another stop they bought 50 or 100 acres of land; they also got brownies from this established family. At the buffalo hunter's brush arbor they traded soap for buffalo jerky, and the Texas Rangers paid off the Comancheros in scrip for their troubles of ransoming the white captives from the Comanches. The Comanches traded beads for pemmican, and they also had a white captive they were willing to ransom if people had enough trade goods. The Goodnights passed out water from their well. Students saw what they got for their money and what they gave up in exchange. Students looked at the human cost of ransoming captives and the role of governments in these exchanges. When looking at intermediaries, students examined the idea of profit as each transaction passed on the cost of the transaction to the consumer.

CONCLUSIONS

Teachers are always looking for ways to encourage their students to find out more about the diverse people who surround them. Social studies teachers encourage students to develop as democratic citizens in a diverse world. Because this community where the students live and practice democracy is quite diverse, working with a variety of people is very important; as a result of this contrived experience the community got to see members of minority groups included in instruction. Third- and seventh-grade students together learned about multiple peoples, their lifestyles, and their ideas. The history walk allowed students to see that diversity existed from the very beginning of people coming to live in proximity to one another in this area.

Teachers had an opportunity to work in cross-grade teams to develop curriculum for students who learn and work together. Third-grade students got to work with big ideas and made connections with their previous learning that deepened their understanding of a specific time period. Seventh-grade students got to teach economics concepts to students and became involved in an economic simulation and a re-creation of a time period. Social studies teachers need to teach citizens how to work across various age levels as the population becomes more mature, the community got to see the seventh-grade students in a leadership role with the third-grade students. When people work across age levels, they must listen to one another and work together in order to teach one another.

The interdisciplinary nature of the social studies allowed third-grade students to talk on some topics when integrated that they would never have examined without this stimulus. Social studies teachers need to help students understand the interconnected nature of social problems of the past with those of today's world. Seventh-grade students improved their understanding of living conditions by recreating the situation for others. Teachers covered more material in greater depth through interdisciplinary teaching, and the community members got important social understanding from integrated instruction. Teachers and learners did not carve content into small, distinct pockets of knowledge, but rather they looked at overlaying themes.

Drama provided a social studies platform for talking about important ideas and issues from the past as well as those in the present. Third-grade students became intimately associated with the situation, and seventh-grade students experienced relearning and interpreting a time period for others. Teachers have opportunities to get students to think about how they will present material to others. To do this they must seize the project by making the process theirs; students cannot be passive when involved in drama. The active engagement of the students helps them focus and think about what they are learning while they are involved with the project. The community needs to see that students can do great things when they are afforded the opportunity and the encouragement to make a difference, especially while learning about the past.

Thought Questions

1. How can first-person presentations incorporate multicultural content or demonstrate interaction between multiple groups?
2. How can audiences participate with first-person reenactors in programs?
3. What interactions can be shown between first-person presenters in a group or between groups?

Note

1.   Morris, Ronald V. (2000). The History Walk: Integrated Multi-Age Learning. *Gifted Child Today*, 24(4), 22–27, 53. Reprinted with the permission of Prufrock Press Inc. (http://www.prufrock.com)

References

Banks, J. (1991). Multicultural education: Its effects on students' racial and gender role attitudes. In J. P. Shaver (Ed.), *Handbook of research on social studies teaching and learning* (pp. 459–469). New York: Macmillan.

Brophy J., & Van Sledright, B. (1997). *Teaching and learning history in elementary schools*. New York: Teachers College Press.

Fines, J., & Verrier, R. (1974). *The drama of history: An experiment in cooperative teaching*. London: New University Education.

Gandy, S. K. (2007). Connections to the past: Creating time detectives with archaeology. *Social Education*, 71(5), 267–271.

Goalen P., & Hendy, L. (1993). 'It's not just fun, it works!' Developing children's historical thinking through drama. *Curriculum Journal*, 4(3), 363–384.

Kelin, D. A., II. (2005). Voyages of discovery: Experiencing the emotion of history. *Social   Studies and the Young Learner*, 18(1), 7–10.

Marri, A. R. (2005). Building a framework for classroom-based multicultural democratic education: Learning from three skilled teachers. *Teachers College Record*, 107(5), 1036–1059.

Millward, R. (2007). Rope circles and giant trees: Making history come alive. *Social Studies and the Young Learner*, 19(3), 18–19.

Morris, R. V. (2007). Social studies around the blacksmith's forge: Inter-disciplinary teaching and learning. *Social Studies, 98*(3), 99–104.

———. (2000). Teaching social studies with artifacts. *Social Studies, 9*(1), 32–37.

———. (1998). Common threads: How to translate best practices into teaching. *Journal of Social Studies Research, 22*(2), 11–18.

National Council for the Social Studies. (1994). *Expectations of excellence: Curriculum standards for social studies.* Washington, D.C.: Author.

National Council on Economics Educators. (1997). *National Content Standards in Economics.* Washington, D.C.: Author.

Peterson, C. (2004). *Jump back in time: A living history resource.* Portsmouth, NH: Teacher Ideas Press.

Stevens, R. L., & Starkey, M. (2007). Teaching an interdisciplinary unit on shelter. *Social Studies and the Young Learner, 20*(1), 6–10.

Chapter Eight

---○---

First-person in an Eighth Grade United States History Classroom

GLEN DILLMAN USES FIRST-PERSON historical presentation with the members of his four fifty-minute sections of eighth-grade social studies class. He teaches in a rural consolidated school district where the junior/senior high school is located in a small Indiana town. He portrays members from his community who participated in nationally significant events. Glen uses first-person presentation, historical clothing, and artifacts because he finds these methods to be very effective with his students. For more information on historic costumes, see appendix 1. He assumes the character of a person from the past to help his students immerse themselves in the time described. Glen Dillman remembers:

> The very first presentation that I ever tried . . . I told the kids that I had arranged for this English gentleman to come, and he was going to debate [with them], because he was very adamant about what had happened in the American Revolution. [He said] that the Americans were wrong. So I got them to do a lot of research. . . . The day came, and I told them that this guy was coming. . . . He was down at the office. . . . Originally, I said, "You need to research and make sure you can debate [with] him. Because, he is going to debate [with] you on whether it was right or it's wrong, and whether Americans have the right to withdraw from the British Empire." . . . I went down to the office. . . . I put on a cape and I put on a crown. . . . I came into the classroom, and

105

that was really the very first characterization. . . . They had done a lot of research, and I was really impressed. It really . . . was very interactive, and I became the debater with them.

RATIONALE

Using first-person historical presentations oftentimes requires a teacher to use substantial artifacts in the construction of their presentation. These artifacts help make an initial connection with the students, and the students quickly focus their attention on the artifacts and the situation. Teachers describe experiences in which their students used artifacts to learn historical knowledge (Millward, 2007; Ruder, 2005) and thinking skills (Easley, 2005; Yell, 1998). Students use artifacts to gain a curiosity about what they want to study, and then by exploring along the lines of their interests the students motivate themselves to discover more about the topic. Middle-school students learn about social studies through the use of artifacts in their instruction. Regardless of the content students dive into artifacts to find out about the people and places in their social studies class.

When middle-school students engage in dramatic and role-playing experiences in social studies class, they work with historical concepts and engage in multiple techniques to learn more about the subject. All of the students find themselves engaged with the events they explore in their classroom. Some students work with inquiry techniques (Akmal & Ayre-Svingern, 2002; White, O'Brien, Smith, Mortensen, & Hileman, 2006), or narrative (Bianchetti, 2004), and others work with decision-making skills (Corum, 2004). Drama and role-playing bring middle-school students into the action rather than passively experiencing the classroom events. Students make connections to local history and national trends or international events. In all of the classrooms teachers help students make good decisions through decision-making experiences and attempt to connect them to positive citizenship skills with application to society.

The results of middle-school students working with role-playing and drama are manifested in a variety of areas. The result of using drama to learn social studies depends on the questions asked in the study. While some observers focus on student question generation (Mattioli & Drake, 1999), others examine the meanings that students construct (Morris, 2001), and yet others determine affective response and retention (Otten, Stigler, Woodward, & Staley, 2004). By determining students' affective response and retention to history, their future achievement in history can be predicted. All of these studies observed the integration of the humanities into the social studies curriculum through music, drama, and literature. The students exhibited historical thinking in their work, including such skills as problem solving, analysis, and decision making.

Glen Dillman tries to find local people who have experienced history in order to show the students that history is not just a subject in a dusty old book that one merely carries around. History is right around the corner from you. For example, Dillman's next-door neighbor was shot at, and the guy standing next to him was killed at Kent State University. The man who carried the trigger parts to the airplane for the atomic bomb died recently in Carroll County. History is made up of people who are all around us. If teachers help their students find those people in the community, the students realize this is a very intimately connected giant jigsaw puzzle. Glen wants his students to understand history by how they fit into it. Glen says:

> I grew up hearing my grandfather tell the stories about how his part of the family came to America. I can still remember his telling stories about [how] his father was born on the boat coming to America, and how his father's father died three days out from New Orleans. . . . I remember hearing those family stories . . . and . . . as I grew up interested in those stories those stories hooked me on history. . . . I wanted to understand how I was a piece of the whole puzzle of the whole part of American . . . and world history. . . . Why our German family was leaving Alsace-Lorraine and coming to America. They did not want their little boys to have to grow up to be soldiers, and they wanted to come here. . . . My great great grandmother got kicked off the canal boat in Logansport with two little boys, . . . an infant, and no [husband] because she did not have any money to go further. . . . She ended up in Logansport. . . . She ended up marrying a guy, and how the

man she married . . . [owned the land] where my mother . . . lives today. . . [If] everyone of them . . . can get that idea of, "Why am I here?" and "How am I a part of this story?" not that one is better than another . . . but I think that is what social studies is about, "Who am I?" . . . "How do I value myself ?" . . . "Where are we today?" "How we got here?" and "Where are we going?" I have enough years under my belt now that I attended a funeral this last week. . . . Some of my former students from twenty-five and thirty years ago were there, and some of them came up and talked about lessons . . . we had done twenty-five and thirty years ago that still impact them today. I think it is really important that the lessons we have not just teach facts, but they teach a story. They teach America: "Who am I?" . . . "How have I grown?" That is what social studies is about; we study society.

Glen Dillman thinks that showing students the pieces of the puzzle reveals the mosaic of American history and how his students all fit together.

PROCEDURE

Glen Dillman has always taught social studies standards even though he started using first-person historical presentations before the creation of the standards. He has also always taught with objectives and concepts. Glen says,

This is just another road to get those covered; it is just a little more scenic on this road. . . . . When you look at the road maps some of the road maps . . . have the double red line . . . the big black line, and sometimes you have the little green line that wiggles all over the place. This is one of those little green scenic tour roads.

Even though Glen talks about teaching history he works in an interdisciplinary format interweaving economics, geography, history, and political science into his first-person presentations as he incorporates National Council for the Social Studies standards (1994) [see appendix II]:

II. Time, Continuity, and Change
III. People, Places, and Environments
VI. Power, Authority, and Governance
VII. Production, Consumption, and Distribution

Glen wants his students to have an open mind to examine ideas from several different vantage points. He helps his students meet lots of different people from history with lots of different perspectives to help his students see that there is not just one vantage point.

By informing and preparing his principal in advance, Dillman does not surprise him by just walking into school one day in a weird outfit. When he first thought of doing a first-person historical presentation, he went to his principal and said that he had an idea on how to make his classes even better. He wanted to dress in historical clothing, and the principal gave him the freedom to do this with responsibility. The principal said, "Oh, I trust your judgment that you know that if it works fine and if it doesn't then you move on to something else." Glen took this opportunity and when the students responded to it, he built on it in future years. He had administrative support, or at least toleration, for his ideas. Glen thinks that it is very important that he did not just go in and start doing something and then have parents say, "What the heck is this? What is going on here?" Contact with the administration headed off questions from the community. He is not afraid to look for support among multiple administrators. When teaching in a small school district, one can prepare the principal and maybe even the superintendent, by saying, "I am going to try this, and if it doesn't work I am going to give it up—no differently from any other technique we might try." His willingness to experiment to see what would work well with his students in this community has served him well with both the parents and administrators with whom he has worked. Once he built a reputation for being a creative teacher in this small community, he had lots of support.

Glen is emphatic about where the preparation needs to be placed in creating a presentation. The facts must be correct, and they need to support thoughtful interpretation of history. Glen says, "There is no substitute for knowledge. Because if you get a great costume and you do not have anything to say you are just a bumbling idiot in front of a bunch of kids while looking funny." He thinks the most important part of the presentation is the information one presents to the students. He has no time to waste for entertainment or entertainers. He has serious mission-driven social studies experiences he wants to share with his students.

Dillman once attended a workshop where his friend Kevin presented a first-person presentation to a group of teachers. It had been a multiple-presentation week for Kevin on top of a throat infection, which left him with just a shadow of his normal voice. Kevin asked Glen, who was sitting in the back row in a suit and tie, to comment. Glen stood and started moving forward through the group giving a small segment of the Lewis and Clark first-person presentation. After the first fifteen seconds, it did not matter what Glen wore; the teachers focused on what he was saying and he was in character. Neither Kevin nor Glen knew this was going to happen, but it really showed the teachers that it is the power of the method rather than the clothing that gets the point across.

One drawback to this method is the huge amount of resources and time that goes into researching and creating this type of presentation. If it is going to be a quality program, it takes a lot of time to prepare, check facts, and get it polished for presentation. Glen Dillman sets aside three to five hours to study and refresh himself for the details of the presentation. There is also set-up time for the presentation to arrange the props. Glen comments that early access to the Internet would have made researching these characters a lot easier. "There is so much . . . available from libraries and museums now that it is overwhelming."

He always prepares the students for the approaching experience. One time he did not prepare a class well enough and that taught him that he needed to always prepare his students. He tells them what he is going to do, when he is doing it for them, and why they should not mess it up for everybody. He has never had to stop a presentation in the middle of a program. He tells the students a little about the person who is coming to visit the next day, and Glen points out that there are some things that he cannot change about himself. He can neither change his height, his weight, nor the fillings in his teeth. He can, however, present content information to his students in a way that makes them have a better experience in class and helps them better understand what occurred in history. Before the presentations he also gives them an outline of major points in the presentation to help them identify major themes.

Glen observes that most students become very fascinated with first-person presentations and therefore learn to appreciate them. They are viewing it as a window into the past. It is an opportunity for them to interact with somebody from history and to learn from that person. He thinks it is much better if the students can ask questions. He does not seed the audience with questions, but he tries to get particular students to interact with a story line. Further, when the students are asking questions about the presentation, they have a natural curiosity that will help them remember information. Glen likes to interact with the students so it is not merely a performance. He believes that the great thing about first-person presentation is that the students realize how special it becomes.

Glen Dillman does not use any notes when he is in front of the class because he believes that he needs to know the material as if he were the person. It is his character telling the story, and he becomes that person communicating directly to the audience. That is not to say that he cannot "seed the set"; there can be a card out of sight of the audience with a word or a phrase to spark a memory of where to go next. Normally though when he gets to the place where he needs to go on to the next point, he just looks around at all of his props and there are all of those things that would provide clues as to where to go with the next story. Students' questions and comments also shape the route of the presentation.

When Glen Dillman presents, he makes critically important eye contact, and he tries to meet every student's eye in the room once every minute or two. Glen monitors the students with constant eye contact, and he looks directly at them. He focuses his attention on them and even gets down on his knees or hunches over to talk to them directly. He often has an intimate conversation with one person, while everybody else just eavesdrops on the conversation. The other students never know when he is going to be in front of them in two or three minutes.

Glen moves. He moves around using gestures, picks up props, and refers to a map. One of the items for the front board is a map that shows the gold rush across California, Arizona, and New Mexico. He uses voice inflection, and he yells, "Gold, there's gold in them hills." When he enters a room he likes to seize on the uncertainty of the situation, "What are you doing on my campsite?" The students all look around dazed and confused by the character dressed like a miner addressing them in such a manner. He not only repeats but goes further, "What are you doing on my campsite? Can't you see those markers over there? See that marker?" By being slightly confrontational Glen introduces an element of uncertainty and doubt that the students must resolve in order to determine what is occurring. The students, while still being perplexed, discern a little tin can; inside the can is the marker for his campsite. Glen addresses them again, "Well, you must be a bunch of greenhorns? Are you just getting here? How did you get here?" Glen directs their conversation to how he got there, how long it took, the things he saw on the way, and why he came west. Glen does not stay in one place, he keeps coming back to the students wherever they are seated, and he constantly keeps moving. The demonstrative nature of the presentation, the pacing, the confrontation as introduction, and the initial engagement in determining how the students got to the goldfields hooks the students' interest immediately.

Glen says that the first-person presentation is never perfected. He continues to experiment, improve, and tinker with ways to engage students in the presentation. "The first time you do it you say, "I have got to do these certain things; I have an agenda." Then he keeps polishing and adding to it. He continues to look for ways to update and improve student response to the presentations.

> It is like your house. You keep adding this and that, . . . tweaking, and making it better. . . . I don't think there is ever a final way of getting it done right . . . They grow.

There is always another piece of information to add. There is always another introduction or debate to try. By never being complacent, there is always room for creative teachers to experiment and up-grade.

Do Not Be Afraid to Walk Away

Glen Dillman is emphatic that if he ever finds something that works better with his students than first-person presentations, he will use that method. He would not continue to use first-person presentations just because he has developed a character. One year Glen Dillman created a character by the name of Manassa Cutler, who was actually a congressman in the early United States legislature, and a local town was named in his honor. He put a lot of research into it, but Glen realized the character just did not attract the interest of the students so he abandoned that character and selected a method that was more powerful to teach about that content. Glen created other first-person presentations that he retired due to the realignment of the eighth-grade curriculum covering all of United States history from European Contact to Reconstruction. He thought about developing a Reconstruction character but dropped it. He retired a soldier with Captain Jack from the Modoc Indian war, a Spanish-American War soldier, a World War I soldier, a stockbroker from the 1929 stock market crash, and a World War II soldier. There are always new media and new ways of dealing with ideas. For Glen, first-person presentation is no different from using filmstrips, films, DVD, lecturing, or doing a class play. It is just another means of communicating content. There are still 180 days in which students must investigate material, so he cuts all of the frivolous things from the curriculum.

When Glen does a first-person presentation, he usually works with his students alone; however, he has had student teachers who have joined him in the presentations. One female student teacher got a dress and hoop skirt and just dived right into the presentation as a slave owner. Her brother was in the state militia. Glen thinks that it is actually harder to do first-person presentations with two people, because when two people are talking back and forth there is less time for the audience to interact with the presenter. The danger is for the two teachers to talk to each other and crowd out the students; often the students sit back and watch rather than dive in to participate.

Comparing Students

Glen believes that the student who benefits the most from a first-person presentation is the junior high/middle school student. If they are prepared, know the purpose, and the assessment outcomes, they are best equipped to profit from the method. They have the temperament to interact with the presenter, but they also now have enough background experiences to ask probing questions. They can use the knowledge they acquire to create elaborate communication in written essays or projects. They are playful enough to enjoy the novelty of the method with their peers.

The prevalence of wax museums, in which elementary students do first-person presentations for their peers in elementary school, means that students need models who can do first-person presentations. When Glen works with elementary students, the first thing he notices is the difference in duration of attention span. While the typical middle-school student engages with the first-person character for fifty minutes, the typical elementary student interacts with a first-person character between twenty and thirty minutes. Within that twenty to thirty minutes, two or three activities may need to occur. This means that the depth of content can easily become shallow, and without careful elaboration on major ideas student interest could wane prior to getting to those major ideas.

When Glen Dillman works with an elementary classroom, he notices a lack of preparation for the first-person presentation. The elementary teachers need to help the elementary students understand how to play along with the guest speaker, and the elementary teachers need to help their students understand that Glen will have some things that look slightly similar to things the students are familiar with in their life. One of the most problematic comments from elementary students is, "Oh, my Daddy has a artifact like that." This comment leaves Glen with nowhere to go in entering a new story. He cannot really talk about the student's life or family, and it is hard to get back to a story line. Glen does require that if he is doing a program in another class that the students get the picture frame assignment so he can determine what the students are taking away from the experience.

High school students are almost too sophisticated to enjoy the method. He does not do very much with first-person presentations in his world history class, but most of the students in the school system experienced this method when they were in his eighth-grade class. He does one first-person presentation per year for his high-school world history class, and everyone knows what to expect. When impersonating Martin Luther, he nails a copy of the ninety-five theses to the front board and tells what happened in Martin Luther's life. Even though he does not usually interpret famous characters, this is his exception; the students seem to have a pretty good appreciation of Luther after the event.

Assessment

After a first-person presentation Glen asks his students for a written response about what they learned. The students write a newspaper page as if the Lewis and Clark Corps of Discovery has just returned, and they had an interview with one of the people from the expedition. They write what they saw on this day, but sometimes the students write a first-person account journal or diary entry. Glen knows that not all of his students like to do each type of assignment, so he gives them choices on ways to demonstrate what they have learned. This helps the students make their best case for how much they have learned.

The student's favorite response is to create a series of pictures with captions. He has a paper with picture frames and about five lines for captions, and the students have to draw something they remember from the presentation and then describe it as a form of note-taking. When looking at the picture and caption follow-up assignment, Glen finds it absolutely amazing the things that the students pick up. He may say one small thing that he did not think anybody noticed, and somebody took the time to draw a picture, illustrate it, and explain it with a caption. "My gosh, I can not believe that they actually caught that." Since there are six picture frames, the students prove that they can both interpret details and major ideas from the presentations.

From there the students engage in an essay test that grows out of the presentations. From the essays, it amazes Glen how many details the students remember; they pick up on the least little story. He thinks that this is because the students are interacting and involved with him rather than viewing his performance like a TV show at the front of the room. For the students he is a character from the past with whom they can converse and ask questions. Students illustrate their essay writing with the same colorful images and experiences they have shared in their social studies classroom.

Students do nine-week projects during which they select to study a special topic and share it with the class through a poster, PowerPoint, or book report. In the first nine weeks no one ever does a first-person presentation even though it is an option; however, once they see Mr. Dillman perform one, students start using him as a model for their own first-person presentations. "I just learned . . . about Sacagawea and the Lewis and Clark expedition . . . and believe it or not I learned it from some of my . . . fellow [students] who were doing a characterization." The number builds across the year with students portraying characters from Davy Crockett, to the architect of the White House, to Sacagawea. Glen said they were so good that he would like to get the students on UTube. Glen was very proud of his students as they completed their latest project.

> They did a wonderful job, and . . . it is a great experience for them. . . . The miracle is [that] at least half of those kids are the kids that I would never in 100 years have picked as the ones that would come out and be the shining star. . . . That is the really neat thing, because it brings out a new personality in somebody. . . . They . . . are learning to fulfill themselves in this vehicle of first-person presentation.

Mr. Dillman does not ask his students to memorize everything like he does. He lets his students use note cards, but he does not allow them to read them. If students want to do something further with their presentations, he figures they will grow into their part.

Problems and Pitfalls

Glen finds the most discouraging thing about the present standards and testing environment is the chilling effect it has had on creative teaching. He feels that creative teachers think outside the box and try new things because they want to help their students. He is committed to teaching history to all of his students, and he appreciates the place of standards. Further, he would confidently compare all of his students to any others in their understanding of history. He is skeptical that standardized tests can measure the sophisticated understandings of history that his students create, and he finds the cost of squeezing interesting experiences out of the curriculum to make time for testing students abhorrent.

The School of Hard Knocks

In the early creation of Glen's first-person presentations he focused so much on gathering research, creating story lines, memorizing it, and preparing historical clothing that he forgot to keep good records. The next year when he came back to do this first-person presentation, he had to start from scratch to re-create the character. From this bad experience he learned to always keep a file of his research notes and to make and keep an outline on file. Glen has all of the research notes for each character he has developed even if he no longer uses that character. It is easy for him to access the information, and it certainly helps to keep him from researching and creating the presentation over again every year.

Warning

One of the first things that the teacher who works with first-person presentations learns is never to show people their personal calendar because when people see blank spaces on a calendar, they try to fill them. When people in the community find out that a teacher does first-person presentations, the presenter then becomes a target for every group program chairperson who is on the prowl. The average civic club member wants to be entertained, but most first-person presentations have little purpose for being performed outside the classroom. Beware of anyone who wants a custom-made first-person presentation. This is an extremely large amount of work that a teacher will probably never be able to adapt to his own classroom.

Glen finds that the problem with doing successful first-person presentation is that requests start coming in for programs at other schools, both within the school district and from other school districts. The problem for Glen is that he still has to teach his own classes. Sometimes people even ask him to use his own personal leave day to do a program for them. He also has to get his props and costume to the site. The first few times he went to the elementary school adjacent to his school, he had to make his own arrangements for a substitute. He has come to the conclusion that he is willing to help people by providing programs, but it is their responsibility to make all of the arrangements for him, including a substitute for his class, transportation of his props to and from the school, and a place and time to change for the presentation.

EXAMPLES

Columbus

Glen Dillman portrays a Columbus expedition member named Diego Mendez. The historical clothing for that character includes a big floppy pair of pants, large shirt, and a little wool hat.

French Fur Trader

When Glen Dillman creates a first-person presentation of a French fur trader, he does not pattern it from one individual. He uses a variety of sources and creates a composite character. The difficulty in finding translated sources from a population that tended to be illiterate is daunting. Glen found a convenient place to gather materials for this first-person presentation, however; just a few miles from his school is the site of a major annual reenactment of this period in time called the Feast of the Hunter's Moon. He uses this location to help his students understand about life in two different cultures over two centuries ago.

With this experience students get to look at geography, history, and economics as they determine what they would trade. They examine purchasing power on the frontier and the notion of even trade between two people who both stood to profit from the exchange. At the first sign from the students that their attention might wander, Glen has them come to the trade blanket and asks them, "What do you want to trade?" In setting up a trade blanket Glen secured a calf skin and a bearskin rug and found mirrors, ribbons, dyes, traps, and pieces of cloth. If Glen has not talked about something the students will ask about it, and that leads to more information about needles, trade beads, gunpowder, and dyes. The students say, "What is that?" Glen says, "Oh, you like those kinds of things. . . ." He tells them what it would take from them to get the item they desire. He selects someone to try on the blanket coat or capote, shows them how to put the hood on, how to tie it all tighter, how to put the buttons on for it, how it is fit just for you, and how much it costs in trade.

> My wife, she made this capote. She is a good Indian. She is good at chewing the leather for the moccasins, and I just happen to have moccasins I can sell to you. I can supply you with the traps, and with these loaned traps you can trap beaver that mean nothing to you. You can bring the beaver skins to me. I will make your life better, and you will make my life better. [Glen intertwines his fingers.] You know we Frenchmen have things for you, and you have things for us. The Indians and the French are like two hands working together. We are not like the Spanish; the Spanish come and they enslave the Indian. The English come, and they drive the Indian away. They take away his wilderness and take away the land. What we do is make your life better. We do not tell you that you have a bad way of life. We dress like you. We marry your women. We make life better.

By creating a fur trader, Glen Dillman shows the bitterness that led to the French and Indian War. The students examine the competing territorial claims of rival nations in the context of a global empire. Century-old rival political and economic systems also clashed on the North American continent.

Glen also has the students play the moccasin game, and he gives three students a coin/button. He takes a coin/button, and he has four moccasins. Glen says, ""I know you Indians like to gamble. There is a button in my hand, and I am going to put it in one of these moccasins. You watch and then you gamble on which one has the coin/button." He puts his hand inside each of the moccasins and drops the coin/button in one of them while being careful not to let the students guess which moccasin contains the coin/button. The moccasin game illustrates the intersection of French and Indian cultures in recreation. Finally, he pulls his hand out of the last moccasin and puts it down before saying, "You gamble on which moccasin holds the coin/button." The students put their coin/button down on the moccasin they think has the coin/button inside. Most of the students will guess the wrong moccasin, and Glen will win the coin/button they put down on the moccasin. If a student guesses correctly, they get the coin/button that Mr. Dillman put inside the moccasin. Glen says, "You Indians are so trustworthy that many of you don't even have a word for "lie" in your languages, but some of you like to gamble so much that some of you will gamble an entire year's work away in an afternoon." Through the experiences of this first-person presentation, students examine Western and non-Western cultures. The students have many more experiences within the first-person presentation than just listening for an hour.

Indentured Servant

When Glen Dillman started with a character from this time period, he portrayed Phillip Fithian. Glen found accounts and account books that placed Fithian on the Carter plantation. Glen did that for a couple of years and then in the 1980s he engaged in some teacher in-service where he found the indentured servant diary of John Harrower. This was nearly perfect for his classroom needs because it described details of everyday life, such as working side by side with the plantation owner and traveling with him, finding snakes in his bed, and being the first person in America to provide a deaf person with an education. The only thing wrong with the diary was that it was about twenty years off what Glen wanted to portray because John Harrower came to America just as the American Revolution was starting. Glen wanted to portray him in 1753 to teach about plantation life, the conditions in the mature American colonies, and the issues leading to the French and Indian War. Glen focused on Harrower's plantation life stories and used other sources to talk about the French and Indian War issues.

Revolutionary War Veteran

Glen Dillman portrays a Revolutionary War veteran, Nathaniel Farmer, who is buried in the same county where Glen teaches. Glen sent away for the Revolutionary War veteran's war records from the National Archives. From that information Glen was able to find out the unit the veteran served with and the time he was with that unit. From there Glen was able to determine where the unit was and what happened to this character. Glen works to connect distant events and places to the world where his students live.

Lewis and Clark

Glen will use anachronistic methods if he thinks his students can learn from them; he knows his students are sophisticated enough to suspend their disbelief for a few minutes. He lets his students know ahead of time, "Yes, I am going to be using slides, but I am doing this for your good." His students take the slides in stride and play along so that they can see into the memories of his character. He does an introduction as Sergeant Patrick Gassed, and then he shows the slides of Lewis and Clark and the Corps of Discovery. Glen wears a hunter's coat, a peace medallion suspended by a ribbon around his neck, a leather bullet bag, and a felt hat; he also carries a diary. He has a student advance the slides, and the slides carry the story forward for him. Glen looks at a picture, and it reminds him of a story, "Oh, I will never forget this day when the bank washed away and the island almost washed out from under us." The adventure, the majesty of the land, and the act of discovery all come through from the pictures even though these eighth-grade students have not seen the West. The students get to visualize the land and sense that every scene was brand new to the explorers. By using technology the students get to see expanses and details they could not have otherwise seen from their classroom.

War of 1812

For several years Glen Dillman portrayed a War of 1812 veteran who had participated in the Battle of New Orleans and was buried in the cemetery about a quarter of a mile from the school where he teaches. He started class in regular clothes and showed a filmstrip about the lead into the War of 1812 that would take about 15 minutes. What the students did not know was that the pants were part of his historical clothing. He stepped into an alcove out of sight of his students to slip on a coat, bullet bag, and hat. At the point where the filmstrip on the War of 1812 got to the Battle of New Orleans, he popped out of the back of the room, turned off the filmstrip, and had the light flipped on. All of a sudden he went from a filmstrip to a person from the Battle of New Orleans, who is actually telling the story of how the British came to fight and how Andy Jackson and the muddy shirts were able to stop them. Glen gave up this presentation when he found better materials, but he says the research he did for that character helped him grow in his knowledge of the time. Even now he incorporates that material into his lessons; even though he is not doing a full first-person characterization, he can still sprinkle the information into his classroom presentation.

First Settler in Carroll County

Every eighth-grade teacher talks about frontier life. If the teacher is going to talk about frontier living, why not talk about the frontier in the students' own county? Glen selected the first settler in the county where he teaches. He researched the character, found all the stories he could locate, and then incorporated that information into how people moved into northern Indiana and Carroll County. It creates a specific connection to the students in his class, and it helps them learn about the broader picture of national history. Glen uses props that he has accumulated over the years for the first settler in the county, including such tools as hoes, shovels, axes, and a bed wrench, which was used to tighten the bed ropes.

The Gold Rush

The gold rush is such an easy topic to research; almost any library has enough information to construct a presentation. Glen creates an outline of information about the gold rush for himself, which he shares with his students. He then enters the classroom after a student shows twenty slides for three seconds each. He turns some of his objectives into questions for the students.

- How did you get to the gold rush?
- Did you come overland?
- Did you go by the shortened route down through Central America?
- Did you go all the way around the horn of South America?
- So how did you get here?

He asks the students questions, and they play along with him.

Glen Dillman observes that if he has a prop, there had better be a good reason for it being there because the students will ask him about it. He has to have a story to accompany it. When the students enter the classroom, Glen has extra clothes that were too small for him to wear so he makes a sign on the front board stating that the clothes are for sale due to the death of the owner; for $150 the purchaser also gets the deceased's shovel and gold pan. He puts up a tent and scatters tin cans around the site. There are three gold pans, an ax, a mattock, and wooden handled shovels standing in a cluster, plus a little vial of gold. Some red long johns hang on a line, and a tripod with a pot, a cooking pan, and a wooden bowl with potatoes, apples, cabbage, eggs, and onions are set on a table at his campsite. Since his character is both a doctor and a gold miner, on top of the table he places his medical bag and hangs his doctor's sign which reads, "Visit to doctor $100 and laudanum $100 per drop." Glen tells his students that depending on the time, an individual egg might cost from three to five dollars in the money of the day, and a head of cabbage costs a dollar. Glen uses some tent canvas over a classroom table to make a tent and creates a bed underneath by using a Mexican blanket.

Glen has a pair of pants from a German Baptist member of the community that are like Levi Strauss jeans with the button drop front and a pair of suspenders. He has a pair of boots and a red shirt. With the kerchief in his pocket, he tells the story about how a boy needed some help and how the gold miners all agreed to dig for an hour for him. Then Glen takes the handkerchief from his pocket and lays it out on a student's desk. Glen pretends he is putting gold in the kerchief and then bunches it up and hands it to one of the students. He wants his students to have the experience of panning for gold so across time he has found three gold pans. After his demonstration the students pan for gold and operate a mining cradle that he has made.

Slave Master

Glen Dillman always prepares his students, but with this character he is exceedingly careful. He tells them that a slave owner is going to talk to them. He does not have a lot of black students, but he does have biracial students. He talks to them beforehand and then makes home contacts to explain what he is going to do; although he really does not believe what this character will be saying, it is an important part of history for the students to understand. This first-person presentation helps students to understand more about the roots of the Civil War and the sectional feeling that dominated antebellum life.

When Glen does his first-person presentation as a slave owner, he describes it as both the hardest as well as the most memorable day of the school year. He wears a cream-colored suit and a paisley vest with a watch and a big Panama hat. His few props include a cane; a gild-edged framed picture of his son Beauregard, who is

presently in the militia; some cotton with the seeds in it; a whip
that just happens to be lying there; a couple of newspapers; and a
map of the South. He justifies slavery and tells his students how
good slavery is for the purpose of getting them to debate with him.
At one point in his career he had his students each select a side
and debate, but it was ignorance debating ignorance. He decided
to become the controversial person, and the students have to come
up with reasons why he is wrong. As the class continues, it ends
up that the students debate the morality of the issues, and the
slave owner debates the economics of the issue. The students and
he are unable to communicate because they are talking at cross-
purposes.

While the class starts out very civilly with the slave owner on a
speaking tour of the North to help them understand the issue and
why the South is preparing to leave the nation, Glen can feel the
frustration building as the debate continues.

> Slavery is a much more human[e] system. I take care of my
> people from the cradle to the grave, and they do not have to pay
> anything for any of their supplies. I give them medical care, and
> if I don't I have lost my entire investment. In the North when
> your Daddy gets laid off does the factory owner give you food
> and medicine? No, he just kicks you out, and you don't have
> anything. Oh don't give me that about the slave owners bringing
> slaves into this country. We have not been allowed to bring slaves
> into this country since 1808, and by the way where did most of
> those slave ships come from that brought the slaves to America?
> They brought slaves to America, they filled your pockets and your
> bank account in the North. Oh, if I am not mistaken, Indiana just
> created a new constitution about seven years ago, and it has a
> provision that you do not allow Blacks to stay in your state. They
> must keep moving; that sounds like hypocrisy to me.

As the debate goes on, the students get more and more agitated.
The students really do not like it when he points his cane at them,
and sometimes when he is emphasizing a point with the cane they
grab at it. He has had students stand up and remove the Confederate flag that is hanging on the blackboard for this lesson and throw
it in the wastebasket. Glen reports that he has even had students

get up to hit him. Usually about five minutes before the end of the period, the anger level is at the stage of yelling back and forth at each other. He backs out of the room telling them, "All you have to do to have peace is just leave us alone and let us leave the nation. Let us create our own nation." Mr. Dillman says, "At that point they are so angry with me [that] I close the door, and they [continue] yelling at full volume. People up and down the hall are wondering, "What is going on in there?" Then he opens the door to return and as he opens the door, the students will still be yelling at him while he says, "No, no, quiet, quiet, quiet, Mr. Dillman is back now. It is 2008. It's Mr. Dillman. Are you upset? Are you angry?" All of the students are saying, "Yeah." Mr. Dillman says, "If you are angry in 2008 guess what it was like in 1861?" When the buzzer rings, and the students leave the room they understand the rising tensions and anger that propelled the nation toward the Civil War. All of the days when he does first-person presentations are intense, but by the end of the day when he presents the slave owner he is absolutely emotionally and physically exhausted.

Lincoln's Law Partner

The character of William Herndon started by wearing a coat out of Glen Dillman's closet then moved to better and better historical clothing. He now wears a top hat and a pocket watch. The students are fascinated by a ten-dollar ticking pocket watch that actually tells the time. In his pocket he also carries a letter from a little girl who wrote about why Lincoln should grow a beard. He displays four books that influenced Lincoln.

Glen needed a vehicle to teach about Lincoln, but he does not think first-person interpretation works as well if one is attempting to impersonate a famous person like Lincoln. Of course, physically Glen does not look like Lincoln; he is significantly shorter than six feet four inches and rounder than Lincoln's gaunt frame. Glen, therefore, selected William Herndon to impersonate Lincoln because Herndon not only knew Lincoln intimately, but this offered him some distance which allowed Herndon to offer some perspectives on him. This person, who was Lincoln's biographer, allowed the first-person presentation to be heavily documented with primary source material. Story after story from Lincoln or Herndon about Lincoln punctuates the first-person presentation with details from the men themselves.

Civil War Soldier

Glen Dillman interprets Daniel T. Ferrier who won the Congressional Medal of Honor and is buried in the Carroll County town of Camden. Glen has a Union Civil War uniform. He is not a reenactor; he does not dress up on weekends and go out to sleep with his horse. Glen is an educator; everything he does is deliberately designed to help his students learn about the common soldier in the Civil War. Glen tries to shape his first-person historical presentation to reflect both the life of the soldier and life on the home front.

CONCLUSIONS

Glen Dillman's existentialist philosophy of social studies education helps students to decide the following basic questions of their existence including:

- Who am I?
- Where do I fit into my community?
- How do I relate to the United States of America?
- How do I relate to the world?

At the time students are defining themselves through their peers, Glen Dillman helps students to discover their peers across time in the historical community. He works to find local community figures to illustrate national events, trends, and movements. When he helps his students understand that they fit into the community, he also helps them understand that they are connected to people who have directly experienced the event described in their textbooks. Both the students and the people from other times interact because they are related though their association with the United States. He demonstrates not only an existential but also a communitarian philosophy through his teaching, which is developmentally appropriate for his eighth-grade students.

In reflection Glen surmises, "By doing this technique I am able to explain a lot of things and it seems like [that] I can cover so much more in the same amount of time through this vehicle." He believes that the retention level of the students seems to be much better. The essays are always better, and students, who would normally be in the lower levels, do much better with this approach. They are especially able to create complex oral explanations of their learning. Students discover content within a context, they retain the information they get, and this unique method of presentation peaks their curiosity. He sees three advantages to first-person presentations:

1. Context: The students know exactly what is occurring within the narrative.
2. Retention: The students can recall specific examples and overarching themes.
3. Unique: The students find first-person presentations different and unusual.

Teachers are accustomed to competing with mass media, and first-person interpretation is just another way teachers can deliver information to students and help their students engage in learning. The students know how they connect to the context of the presentations. They recall information they have been exposed to, and the element of novelty excites interest from the students. Dillman finds great rewards in helping all of his students to achieve in social studies class by using this method.

Glen Dillman helps his students understand what happened in history as he shares historical events with them. In these first-person presentations he invites his students into the past as both observers and participants. From these unfolding events students learn content and construct historical understanding. Glen reports that students say,

"When is the next one?" "When is our next character coming?" Or "Boy, I sure do remember that." And you know years later I will even have kids see me walking down the hallway in a costume, and they will say, "Which one is this?" Or "Who are you today?" That is the normal question, and you just have to share that with them. "Oh yeah, I remember that one!"

Certainly students remember meeting a person from the past. Middle-school teachers and students work with similar experiences regardless of the level of the students.

THOUGHT QUESTIONS

1. How much difference is there between first-person presentations for second- and eighth-grade students?
2. How do teachers involve eighth-grade students in first-person presentations?
3. Do you agree with Dillman's critique of elementary student and first-person presentation?

REFERENCES

Akmal, T. T., & Ayre-Svingen, B. (2002). Integrated biographical inquiry: A student-centered approach to learning. *Social Studies, 93*(6), 272–276.

Bianchetti, A. (2004). Teaching history in a post-industrial age. *Social Education, 68*(5), S2.

Corum, B. (2004). The essential rule: Do the right thing. *Middle Ground, 8*(2), 24.

Easley, L. M. (2005). Cemeteries as science labs. *Science Scope, 29*(3), 28–32.

Mattioli, D. J., & Drake, F. (1999). Acting out history from the Ice Age to the Modern Age. *Social Studies and the Young Learner, 11*(3), 9–11.

Millward, R. (2007). Rope circles and giant trees: Making history come alive. *Social Studies and the Young Learner, 19*(3), 15, 18–19.

Morris, R. V. (2001). Drama and authentic assessment in a social studies classroom. *Social Studies, 92*(1), 41–44.

National Council for the Social Studies. (1994). *Expectations of excellence: Curriculum standards for social studies.* Washington, D.C.: Author.

Otten, M., Stigler, J. W., Woodward, J. A., & Staley, L. (2004). Performing history: The effects of a dramatic art-based history program on student achievement and enjoyment. *Theory and Research in Social Education, 32*(2), 187–212.

Ruder, R. (2005). Integrating the study of the Holocaust: One school's triumph. *Middle Ground, 9*(2), 28–29.

White, S. H., O'Brien, J. E., Smith, A., Mortensen, D., & Hileman, K. (2006). A history lab environment in the classroom brings the standards to life. *Middle School Journal, 37*(4), 4–10.

Yell, M. M. (1998). The time before history: Thinking like an archaeologist. *Social Education, 62*(1), 27–31.

Chapter Nine

―――――――――――○―――――――――――

Conclusions

SOCIAL STUDIES TEACHERS work with their students to help their students learn citizenship education. Students grow in their understanding of what it means to be an active and contributing citizen. Teachers attempt to actively convey a sense of democracy through both the individuals and the groups that contribute to that democracy. In a democracy it is imperative that students learn and practice knowledge, skills, values, and dispositions that perpetuate democratic society and traditions. Through first-person presentations teachers expose students to citizenship education in a democracy.

Many times teachers work within their community whether it is defined as their classroom, school, or the extended area. Teachers help their students connect to the community for the good of the community. They help their students define community actions that they can take and define civic actions that improve the quality of life in the community. These actions are not always political involvement, but they are many times service-learning projects that connect students' work with both community need and the students' academic content. Many of these projects involve the students in communitarianism where they see the needs of the community and learn to value the interactions of the group. Students working within communities meet peers with like minds and parallel interests irrespective of chronological age.

CONTROVERSIAL ISSUES

As teachers and students explore the history of their community, they invariably encounter controversial issues. When examining the key events where people intersect or where interests collide, it is important for teachers to help students see that each side has a point of view. By exposing the students to the multiple perspectives held by the different people who are involved in the event, students learn that historical discussions are rich in material useful in interpretation of those same events. When students research history, they use multiple sources of varying viewpoints that confirm and disconfirm their narrative. The diversity of thought extends beyond majority opinion to include minority opinion and multiethnic opinions of events.

As teachers and students examine issue-centered social studies, they look at long-enduring problems within democracy and attempt to solve those problems. The average American citizen may long ignore social problems exposed by a history of minority struggle. When students consider issues of social justice, they explore remedies for social inequalities by exploring historical and modern cases. These explorations require students to use thinking skills to analyze, synthesize, and evaluate competing claims and render complex judgments. The act of becoming decision-makers helps students examine long-term problems and render judgments about them.

SOCIAL STUDIES TEACHING

When teaching social studies through first-person presentation, teachers help their students identify social studies concepts. Teachers create objectives for their first-person lessons based on national standards for social studies instruction. Social studies teachers work with parents to help provide experiences for students that extend beyond the walls of the classroom. Teachers use first-person presentations to bring dynamic social studies experiences and situations to their students. Social studies teachers use first-person presentations to help their students answer existential questions about how the student relates to the past and to the present.

Teachers provide opportunities for student assessment beyond the minimum competencies examined through state standardized testing. They ask their students to demonstrate retention of material, and students seem to remember the content due to the unique experience provided by first-person presentations. Students demonstrate their command of their knowledge by exercising elaborate communication in the form of written and oral expression. Further, the members of the community assess the students and community evaluation results when students work with community members or perform in a public space. Community evaluation and approval exercises a powerful motivating force of community recognition and acceptance.

Teachers, who use first-person presentations to teach social studies, participate in five instructional behaviors. First, the teachers immediately gain the attention of their students because the students become interested in the action that is taking place around them. The students then become active participants with the program by interacting with the character, and further involvement devolves from the story line in follow-up lessons and experiences. Second, both the teacher and the students find the process challenging. It is challenging to the teacher, who must engage in creative teaching, and to the students, who must meet and interact with a new figure in the classroom. Further it requires the students to interact with the new character in the presence of their peers, which is more difficult than working one on one with a new character.

Third, the experience of working with a first-person character becomes interdisciplinary for the students. The teacher gathers content from the humanities and the social sciences before arranging it into a presentation using the specific disciplines of geography, history, anthropology, political science, civics, economics, sociology, and psychology. When students respond to the program, it requires them to use elaborate communication skills to question, comment, interact, and evaluate the information they receive from the figure. Since the content is gathered into themes for the purpose of interpretation, the themes can be applicable across grade levels for a variety of student ages. The first-person presentation can also communicate across generations when working with families.

Fourth, the first-person presentation is meaningful to the students who are engaged with it. The first-person presentation allows the students to make a personal connection to some aspect of their life to the character under discussion. By using characters from the community, the students learn more about the people around them. By looking for meaning, the students determine a nexus between themselves and another place or another time. By meeting a first-person character, the students get the opportunity to work with questions of existentialism.

Finally, the first-person presentations allow students to work with values. They examine the values of the character, compare them to their own values, and accept or reject them. In discussing values in this context, the teacher asks the students to examine five different ideas:

- Controversial issues: the condition when two good values compete. How do people show both sides as pros and cons?
- Historical empathy: identify with a figure different from him or her. How does the student make a personal connection with a figure at a different time or place?
- Moral judgment: determine a position on a situation. Is a situation good or bad for individuals, small groups, or all people?
- Multiple perspectives: examine more than one perspective on an event. Who has a different opinion of why these events occurred?
- Social justice: consider providing a better life for all people. Are people working for equality?

Teachers ask students to examine controversial issues as content knowledge, and teachers follow this with skills in the examination of multiple perspectives. Teachers ask students to examine the idea of social justice as content knowledge, and teachers ask students to follow this with the skill of moral judgment. Teachers ask students to examine the idea of historical empathy as content knowledge and the skill of determining social justice for groups of people.

Teachers ask students to examine multiple perspectives as content knowledge, and teachers follow this with skills of historical empathy. Teachers ask students to examine moral judgment as content knowledge, and teachers follow this with skills in the examination of controversial issues.

The students find enough meaning in a first-person presentation so it does not just remain a school endeavor; students carry their interest in these figures into their extracurricular experiences. When the students find that they have enough interest in a subject to turn it into a recreational pleasure, they personalize their learning and carry it into their extracurricular lives. Usually these students will find an informal mentor to work with when producing a first-person presentation. Hopefully, the students will also find a supportive peer group that has like-minded interests. With both a mentor and a peer group, the student who carries extracurricular social studies interests forward will find personal exploration of social studies to be vastly rewarding.

TEACHING HISTORY

When teaching history to their students by using first-person historical presentations, teachers help the students by presenting plenty of context for understanding of circumstances. The teacher provides historical context both with local history and connection to other events that the students understand. The teacher also provides opportunities for deep learning of historical content as well as skills, including both historical knowledge and the ability to create historical narrative. Moreover, the teacher includes social history, the history of the common person rather than the powerful, rich, and famous, and many times includes the history of their own community. Further, first-person presentations are an excellent way to learn about biography as meaningful historic characters illustrate the period of time, and as a way to forge an empathetic bond with people from another time or place. The teacher also engages the students in historical thinking as the students work with the first-person presentation.

When students use inquiry to construct their own first-person presentations or to respond to a first-person presentation, they own the question. It is their quest for knowledge rather than a question imposed upon them by a teacher or a curriculum. When students begin the inquiry process, they explore multiple stages; their discussion often starts with an experience, such as a guest speaker or a field trip. This experience raises uncertainty and doubts in their minds about the amount of knowledge they possess and therefore provides topics they may wish to explore. The desire of the students to find out more leads them to a questioning phase where they create a series of guiding open-ended questions that helps them to define the scope of their research. Based on their questions, students then engage in an interaction between source material; students can use primary or secondary sources to gather information in addition to locating artifacts. These sources will lead them into a debate with their peers and teacher about the merits of the sources, how the sources speak to them, and how the sources shape their finished product. The finished product, which the student creates, is dependent upon their perspective in the interpretation of the data, which they found from their inquiry. Their product may require a complex oral explanation or sophisticated writing provided by the student in order to interpret their work. After the community views the student's work and the members of the community judge the work as meritorious, the student needs to experience the recognition of the community through a form of celebration. This recognition could take the form of news coverage, a reception, awards, and thanks to the members of the community who assisted or contributed to the project. This celebration and the ensuing reflection about the project lead the students to consider the next inquiry project.

In conclusion the teachers of social studies curriculum use drama in the classroom to discover more about history. The teachers, who use first-person historical presentation, introduce their students to a multiple sensory experience through their first-person presentations. The teacher can engage the students further through drama by having the students involved in role-playing events and re-enactments. In re-enactment events students immerse themselves in a re-created series of experiences in time. Through dramatic narrative students learn about their lives and the lives of others across time and space.

THOUGHT QUESTIONS

1. Do you think you could perform a first-person presentation?
2. What would be the greatest impediment to your achieving a successful interpreting?
3. What would you need to do to adapt first-person presentation to people older than eighth-grade students?

Appendix I

———————O———————

Historical Clothing

There are lots of clothes still being produced that are very similar to historical clothing. It was toward the end of the school year I believe, and I was standing in my closet deciding what I was going to wear that day. At school I was going to talk about Lincoln, and as I was going through the closet I found a[n] old black top coat . . . as I was . . . moving through the clothes I was saying, "Oh, top coat, oh my! This looks like a Lincoln coat!" . . . I got to thinking, "Well how can I make a tie?" I think Marti cut a tie down [to size] and [I] just used a regular white shirt . . . so the original costumes were not the greatest, but those things kind of grow with time. You get better and better things.

GLEN HAS BEEN FORTUNATE THAT HIS WIFE, Marti, is a very talented seamstress; Glen found a coat that had the proper lapels for Lincoln's law partner at a thrift shop. Marti cut the sleeves off it and made a whole new back for it. Glen Dillman modifies clothes to make them into what he needs; he swears by Velcro because he can Velcro ties together rather than retying them for each performance. When a quick preparation is needed for the next class, he just touches the Velcro together, and it holds in place. Velcro can adjust the historic clothing, too. In several of the pieces of historical clothing that he wears, his wife has modified clothes by removing collars. For the Revolutionary War, Marti took a blue army coat and remade it by putting facings on the front.

Glen has gone in some different directions based on the needs of creating first-person presentations in his classroom. For example, Glen has his lens prescription placed in original period glasses frames. He removed the brim from an old wool hat to make his Columbus sailor hat. There are lots of different kinds of hats, but since first-person characters are usually done in the classroom, this is one area where he can cut costs. He has also learned to sew leather to create a bullet bag for the first-person presentation for the Lewis and Clark expedition.

Shoes are a problem for him because standing too long on concrete floors, especially in moccasins, is a real killer. Many times he has his pants long enough so that they cover his shoes and dark black or brown shoes look good enough to pass. People do not stare at a presenter's feet as long as he is not wearing something really obvious such as tennis shoes. For the pair of shoes worn by the indentured servant, he adds a pair of costume buckles to the front of an old pair of shoes that he once wore on a daily basis. A comfortable pair of shoes in disguise is more pragmatic than accurate but uncomfortable footwear.

Glen finds lots of places to discover clothing; for example, he found his red shirts for the gold miner presentation at Goodwill. He looks for easily modified clothing, and he tries to remain authentic so he discounts zippers. One resource for Glen is at local reenactments where people are getting rid of old historical clothing. He finds patterns for historic clothing, and he gets information about historical clothing from companies such as James Townsend and Son. Rental clothing is another option. His favorite place to find historic clothing is at yard sales. Glen went to a yard sale and found a beaded chest protector that he can use when talking about Plains Indians. He found his Spanish-American War coat at a yard sale. It was not original, but it was simply a coat with the same cut and material. It looked exactly like the volunteer coats once Marty changed the buttons.

Some of the most expensive clothes Glen owns are some pieces of historic clothing. For the first settler in Carroll County Glen needed some pants that looked like brown linen. He found some drapery material that was the right texture, and he hired a person to make it into pants. Similarly, the members of a church asked him to create a first-person presentation of a circuit rider, and they helped him rent a costume. He made the comment to one of the ladies of the church, "I sure would like to have an outfit like this." She said, "If you find the material I will make you an outfit." Glen still uses that historical clothing since different parts of the clothing works for different characters such as the indentured servant.

Changing clothes on a middle-school schedule can be difficult. Glen needs a place to store clothes and a place where he can change clothes where people will not walk in on him. Glen tries to have the historic clothing on prior to the beginning of the school day. Another problem with using historical clothing at the middle-school level is when the schedule has a different class meeting between the classes that require historical clothing. At one time Glen had three eighth-grade classes, then a world history class, and finally the last eighth-grade U.S. history class. Teaching a world history class in historical clothing appropriate for an eighth-grade U.S. history class was a distraction for those students.

Appendix II

---○---

National Council for the Social Studies Standards

I.   Culture
II.   Time, Continuity, and Change
III. People, Places, and Environments
IV.   Individual Development and Identity
V.   Individuals, Groups, and Institutions
VI.   Power, Authority, and Governance
VII. Production, Distribution, and Consumption
VIII. Science, Technology, and Society
IX.   Global Connections
X.   Civic Ideals and Practices

Index

About the Author

Ronald Vaughan Morris began his career in social studies as a small child traveling with his family to visit historical sites and museums. He continued his love of social studies into adulthood earning a bachelor's degree in elementary education with an endorsement in junior high and middle school social studies, a master's degree in educational psychology and gifted education from Purdue University, and a doctorate of philosophy in curriculum and instruction focusing on social studies education at Purdue University. He currently serves as a professor in the Department of History at Ball State University where he prepares pre-service and graduate elementary social studies students. He is the co-author of *50 Social Studies Strategies for K-8 Classrooms*, and serves at the Ohio River Teaching American History Project Director. The American Association of State and Local History recognized his projects twice with Certificates of Commendations. In 1842 Henry Clay visited a 1830s National Road row house that now serves as the home of Dr. Morris when he is not hiking sections of the Appalachian Trail.

CPSIA information can be obtained at www.ICGtesting.com
Printed in the USA
LVOW081413050213

318750LV00001B/14/P

9 781607 092247